The Bay of Pigs

Christina Fisanick, *Book Editor*

Daniel Leone, *President*
Bonnie Szumski, *Publisher*
Scott Barbour, *Managing Editor*

OPPOSING
VIEWPOINTS®
SERIES

AT ISSUE IN HISTORY

GREENHAVEN
PRESS®

THOMSON

GALE

San Diego • Detroit • New York • San Francisco • Cleveland
New Haven, Conn. • Waterville, Maine • London • Munich

Cover credit: © Hulton/Archive by Getty Images
Library of Congress, 13, 31, 84

LIBRARY OF CONGRESS CATALOGING-IN-PUBLICATION DATA
The Bay of Pigs / Christina Fisanick, book editor.
p. cm. — (At issue in history)
Includes bibliographical references and index.
ISBN 0-7377-1990-7 (pbk. : alk. paper) — ISBN 0-7377-1989-3 (lib. : alk. paper)
1. Cuba—History—Invasion, 1961. 2. Counterrevolutionaries—Cuba—History. 3. United States. Central Intelligence Agency. 4. United States—Foreign relations—1953–1961. 5. International relations—Decision making. 6. Decision making—United States. I. Fisanick, Christina. II. Series.
F1788.B285 2004
972.9106'4—dc21   2003051614

Contents

Chapter 3: The Bay of Pigs Legacy

Foreword

Historian Robert Weiss defines history simply as "a record and interpretation of past events." Both elements—record and interpretation—are necessary, Weiss argues.

> Names, dates, places, and events are the essence of history. But historical writing is not a compendium of facts. It consists of facts placed in a sequence to tell a connected story. A work of history is not merely a story, however. It also must analyze what happened and *why*—that is, it must interpret the past for the reader.

For example, the events of December 7, 1941, that led President Franklin D. Roosevelt to call it "a date which will live in infamy" are fairly well known and straightforward. A force of Japanese planes and submarines launched a torpedo and bombing attack on American military targets in Pearl Harbor, Hawaii. The surprise assault sank five battleships, disabled or sank fourteen additional ships, and left almost twenty-four hundred American soldiers and sailors dead On the following day, the United States formally entered World War II when Congress declared war on Japan.

These facts and consequences were almost immediately communicated to the American people who heard reports about Pearl Harbor and President Roosevelt's response on the radio. All realized that this was an important and pivotal event in American and world history. Yet the news from Pearl Harbor raised many unanswered questions. Why did Japan decide to launch such an offensive? Why were the attackers so successful in catching America by surprise? What did the attack reveal about the two nations, their people, and their leadership? What were its causes, and what were its effects? Political leaders, academic historians, and students look to learn the basic facts of historical events and to read the intepretations of these events by many different sources, both primary and secondary, in order to develop a more complete picture of the event in a historical context.

In the case of Pearl Harbor, several important questions surrounding the event remain in dispute, most notably the role of President Roosevelt. Some historians have blamed his policies for deliberately provoking Japan to attack in order to propel America into World War II; a few have gone so far as to accuse him of knowing of the impending attack but not informing others. Other historians, examining the same event, have exonerated the president of such charges, arguing that the historical evidence does not support such a theory.

The Greenhaven At Issue in History series recognizes that many important historical events have been interpreted differently and in some cases remain shrouded in controversy. Each volume features a collection of articles that focus on a topic that has sparked controversy among eyewitnesses, contemporary observers, and historians. An introductory essay sets the stage for each topic by presenting background and context. Several chapters then examine different facets of the subject at hand with readings chosen for their diversity of opinion. Each selection is preceded by a summary of the author's main points and conclusions. A bibliography is included for those students interested in pursuing further research. An annotated table of contents and thorough index help readers to quickly locate material of interest. Taken together, the contents of each of the volumes in the Greenhaven At Issue in History series will help students become more discriminating and thoughtful readers of history.

Introduction

On April 17, 1961, fourteen hundred CIA-trained Cuban refugees stormed the beaches at Cuba's Bay of Pigs. In less than seventy-two hours most of the men were either killed or captured. The effects of this brief yet bloody battle rippled through the entire world and continues to affect U.S. global relations to this day. According to former U.S. official Howard Hunt, "No event since the communization of China in 1949 has had such a profound effect on the United States and its allies as the defeat of the US-trained Cuban invasion brigade at the Bay of Pigs in 1961."[1]

The events that transpired that day were the culmination of long-term covert planning by the U.S. government and the CIA, which recruited Miami-based Cuban refugees to train in Guatemala for a strike against Cuban leader Fidel Castro. In order to fully understand the impact of this invasion, it is necessary to examine the reasons why the U.S. government felt compelled to devise such a plan in the first place and why these plans failed. Both of these aspects are inextricably linked and reveal a great deal about the workings of the U.S. government during the early 1960s.

Reclaiming U.S. Stakes in Cuba

Just ninety miles off the coast of Florida, Cuba has always been a site of interest for the United States. As early as 1808, when Thomas Jefferson attempted to purchase Cuba from Spain, U.S. leaders have been trying to stake a claim on the island's vast natural resources. Following the Spanish-American War in 1898, Cuba was made a U.S. territory, only to fight for and achieve independence in 1900. Nonetheless, the United States remained heavily involved in Cuban affairs and profited greatly from its sugar, fruit, and molasses production. During the era of Prohibition (1919–1933), when sales and consumption of alcohol were illegal in the United States, Cuba became "the playground of the Caribbean."[2] It remained a posh recreational getaway for the U.S. elite until New Year's Day 1959, when Castro over-

threw Cuban general Fulgencio Batista, who fled to the Dominican Republic.

Although Castro claimed that he was not a Communist,
it became clear in the months following his takeover that he
was in fact planning to make Cuba a Communist state. One
of the leading tenets of communism is equal distribution of
wealth and resources; therefore, Castro's administration began to take over some essential services and goods provided
to the Cuban people, including telephone companies, med-
ication, and housing, and reduced their cost by 30 to 50 percent. He soon began an anti-American campaign with the
intent of reclaiming Cuba's land and resources for the
Cuban people. More than anything, he wanted the Americans out of Cuba.

On May 17, 1959, Cuba enacted the first Agrarian Reform Law, which would limit the amount of Cuban land
that U.S. companies could own. At that time, U.S. sugar
companies owned or controlled over 2 million acres of
Cuban land, and the new reforms would limit U.S.
landownership to 1,000 acres. Needless to say, U.S. officials
were not pleased with Castro's reforms and, in retaliation,
imposed a sugar quota that limited the amount of sugar U.S.
companies could purchase from Cuba. In addition, the U.S.
government refused to sell Cuba arms and prohibited other
countries from doing so as well. These new sanctions hit
Castro hard, but he continued with his reforms, which
prompted the United States to begin bombing sugarcane
fields and other Cuban sites.

Eradicating Communism

Almost immediately after the end of World War II, the U.S.
government began to focus its attention away from the
newly defunct Nazi Germany and made stopping the threat
of communism a top priority. As an increasing number of
Eastern European countries began to adopt communism as
their form of government, the democratic United States felt
alarmed by the possibility of all of these countries uniting.
According to Ellen Schreker, author of *The Age of Mc-
Carthyism: A Brief History with Documents*, each of these governments were "erected under the influence—and backed
by the military presence—of the Soviet Union."[3] Given the
close proximity of the Soviet Union to Alaska, the United
States felt an increasing fear of possible takeover. However,

the United States was even more concerned that if the Communist countries were to unite, they would be led by the Soviet Union.

The U.S. government suspected that Castro and Soviet premier Nikita Khrushchev had an alliance, and this suspicion was confirmed in a June 10, 1960, statement from Khrushchev: "If necessary, Soviet artillerymen can support the Cuban people with their rocket fire if aggressive forces dare to start an intervention against Cuba."[4] With the threat of communism closing in on two sides, the U.S. government felt compelled to take action.

Meanwhile, the U.S. fear of communism intensified and, with the force of Senator Joseph McCarthy, became known as the "Red Scare" because the Communist flag is red. McCarthy accused many Americans, including movie actors, authors, and, later, members of the U.S. government, of being Communist sympathizers and of trying to overthrow the U.S. democratic government. Although many of McCarthy's claims were later disproved, U.S. government officials had already become obsessed with communism and the desperate need to eradicate it from the world.

Ties between Cuba and the Soviet Union further fueled this obsession, and in May 1960 U.S. president Dwight D. Eisenhower secretly ordered Allen Dulles, director of the newly created CIA, to organize and train Cuban exiles for an invasion. The ultimate goal of such an invasion was the ousting of Castro. The U.S. government reasoned that once Castro was gone, then communism in Cuba would also be eliminated. As writer Jason Berry argues,

> The main reason, and possibly the lone reason, for the Bay of Pigs invasion was to stop communism from reaching our country. This meant that the United States government wanted to provoke a counterrevolution in which democracy would be restored and all traces of communism would, subsequently, be destroyed.[5]

Kennedy Inherits the Cuba Problem

Cuba and its Communist threat was one of the primary issues of the 1960 U.S. presidential election. John F. Kennedy used the "Cuban problem" as a platform from which to argue during debates. He insisted that the United States must remove Castro and rid the Caribbean of communism. In an

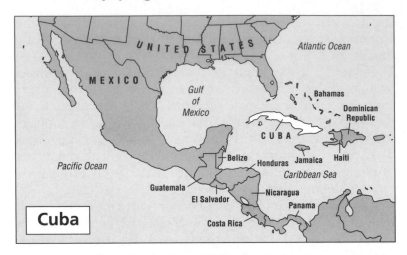

effort to conceal the invasion plans from the American public, Kennedy's opponent, Richard M. Nixon, who had served as vice president under Dwight D. Eisenhower and knew a great deal about these plans, openly denounced an invasion of Cuba, arguing that it would cause major harm to the global perception of the United States.

After winning the election, Kennedy felt that he had to make good on his campaign promise to deal with Castro. Eisenhower briefed Kennedy on the established invasion plans, and Kennedy became ever more obsessed with overthrowing Castro—so obsessed, many historians have argued, that he was unable to make clear, rational decisions regarding the invasion. Although Castro suggested that he was willing to negotiate with the new administration, Kennedy made it clear in his State of the Union address on January 30, 1961, that "communist domination in [the Western] hemisphere can never be negotiated."[6]

Historian Mark J. White offers a somewhat different interpretation of Kennedy's stance on Cuba. In his book *The Cuban Missile Crisis*, White insists that Kennedy's campaign vows to remove Castro from Cuba "delimited his policies as president. To have refrained from the attempt to dislodge Castro, especially when the CIA had a plan ready to go, would have been to renege on an electoral commitment, Cuba would have exposed him to Republican accusations of 'softness' on communism."[7] Whichever the case may be, once Kennedy became committed publicly and privately to ousting Castro, he could not and would not back out.

Divisions Within the Administration

There were two opposing viewpoints within Kennedy's administration concerning the invasion. One side, including members of the State Department and Department of Defense, felt that invading Cuba would not only likely result in failure but would also severely weaken America's reputation around the globe. The other side, mostly composed of the CIA, felt that the invasion was completely sound and that it would be successful in completely overthrowing Castro's regime.

By early February 1961 the Department of Defense had joined forces with the CIA, but the State Department remained opposed to the invasion plans. McGeorge Bundy, the president's special assistant for national security affairs, summed up these opposing views in a memo to President Kennedy:

> Defense and CIA now feel quite enthusiastic about the invasion from Guatemala. At worst, they think the invaders would get into the mountains, and at best they think they might get a full-fledged civil war in which we could then back the anti-Castro forces openly. The State Department takes a much cooler view, primarily because of its belief that the political consequences would be very grave both in the United Nations and in Latin America.[8]

Arthur Schlesinger Jr., President Kennedy's special assistant, was among the most well known and vocal opponents to the invasion. In a memo to the president, Schlesinger wrote that there is no way to conceal U.S. involvement in the Cuban invasion and "at one stroke, it would dissipate all the extraordinary good will which has been rising toward the new Administration through the world."[9]

These conflicting viewpoints presented a major dilemma for the newly elected president, and many historians have argued that his final decision to go forward with the invasion was based on inaccurate information gathered and presented by the recently created CIA. The CIA vastly underestimated the strength, ability, and resources of Castro's militia and was also dealing with interorganizational disagreements. Although at one point Kennedy considered abandoning the plan, he struggled with how to deal with Brigade 2506, the men who were being trained in Guatemala. They would no doubt be confused and angry if the mission were aborted. Many of them wanted Castro out of their country as much as the U.S. government did.

In response to this issue, Richard Bissell, the CIA's deputy director of plans, drafted an opinion paper arguing that although "[Brigade 2506] members will be angry, disillusioned and aggressive . . . and the U.S. will have to face the resulting indignities and embarrassments" if the plans are cancelled, "it may well be considerably less than that resulting from the continuation of the Castro regime or from the more drastic and more attributable actions necessary to accomplish the result at a later date."[10]

In the end, Kennedy made the choice to invade Cuba and the operation failed completely. On April 17, 1961, the CIA-trained Brigade 2506 stormed the coast of Cuba at the Bay of Pigs (*Bahía de Cochones*) and Giron Beach (*Playa Girón*). Within hours, two U.S. ships, the *Houston* and the *Río Escondido*, carrying brigade members and supplies, were sunk by Cuban planes. On land, the brigade suffered many casualties, though some men evaded capture by fleeing to the surrounding swamps. Others waited for promised U.S. support that never came. The CIA had promised the fighting men air support, extra ammunition, and additional weapons, but none of those things materialized. The men felt betrayed and abandoned. At one point, the brigade commander José "Pepe" Peréz San Ramón, asked, "How do these people expect me to defend the beach with no air cover, no artillery, no antiaircraft guns? I'm a military man, not a magician."[11]

Meanwhile, the people of Cuba began attacking Brigade 2506 and effectively fought them off. Their abilities to stop the counterrevolutionaries stunned the CIA, which had fully expected the Cuban people to rise up against Castro. By the next day, the invasion was going so badly that Bissell sent in three bombers to drop napalm and high explosives on the Cuban attackers. Four of the six U.S. pilots were killed. According to the USS *Essex* Association, "One bomber was brought down by anti-aircraft fire over Castro's headquarters at the Central Australia sugar mill. Both pilots survived the crash, but were subsequently shot. The other plane was pursued by a Cuban T-33 and shot down over the sea with the loss of both men."[12] Fighting continued with heavy losses into April 19, when Castro declared that he had won the battle.

In total, more than 1,100 men were captured. Some

died on the way to a holding area, others were shot to death for treason, and the rest were taken to prison. Castro held a mass trial for the surviving 1,189 men and sentenced each one of them to prison for thirty years. In response to pressures from the American people, especially Cuban exiles in Florida and the families of Brigade 2506 members, President Kennedy attempted negotiations with Castro for the release of the captured men. After nearly two years of negotiations, most of the men were released in exchange for $53 million in food and medicine.

After the Invasion

The Bay of Pigs was the biggest blunder of Kennedy's presidency. He was embarrassed and stunned by the loss. Soon after receiving word of the failure, he told veteran and friend Clark Clifford that "this has been the most excruciating period of my life. I doubt my Presidency could survive another catastrophe like this."[13] However, just a year and a half later Kennedy found himself in dire straits over Cuba once again, when he discovered that the Soviet Union had plans to build missile bases there. The Cuban Missile Crisis, as it came to be called, was a direct result of the Bay of

The U.S. fear of the spread of communism in Cuba intensified as Soviet premier Khrushchev (right) declared his support for Castro.

Pigs invasion because the Soviet Union supported Castro, and Premier Khrushchev told Kennedy that he did not agree with his invasion plans. Eventually, the Soviet Union removed its missiles from Cuba, but the possible Cuba–Soviet Union collaboration remained a threat to the United States until the fall of the Soviet Union in 1991.

The Bay of Pigs invasion had long-lasting effects on the Cuban people as well. Some historians, including Victor Andres Triay, argue that it was even more difficult for the Cubans. "Those who supported the Castro regime at the time saw in it a great victory, a validation of their faith in Cuba's new order. For Cubans opposed to Communist rule, the failed invasion represented the end of Cuba's hope for democracy and the initiation of a period of totalitarian, Marxist rule on the island."[14]

Now, more than forty years after the invasion, U.S.-Cuban relations are still fractured. Although some sanctions have been lifted, the United States maintains an embargo on Cuban goods and has restricted trade between Cuba and U.S. allies. For several years educational and religious groups were able to get special travel permits to take groups of U.S. civilians to the island, but even that option has recently been revoked. According to an editorial in the *Columbus Dispatch*, "People have been enjoying these trips too much, administration officials claim, and the cash they spend while having fun under the communist sun undermines the goal of the U.S. embargo, which is to weaken Castro economically."[15] Many independent groups feel that the embargo and travel restrictions only further help Castro control the Cuban people. USA Engage, a group that actively lobbies to end U.S. sanctions against Cuba, argues that such sanctions allow "[Castro] to avoid responsibility for Cuba's failures, blame them on the United States, and solidify control over the Cuban people."[16]

In *At Issue in History: The Bay of Pigs*, the contributors further explore the reasons why the Bay of Pigs invasion plan was developed in the first place, why it failed, and how it has affected U.S. foreign policy and current U.S.-Cuban relations.

Notes

1. Howard Hunt, *Give Us This Day*. New Rochelle, NY: Arlington House, 1973, p. 13.

2. Jane Franklin, *Cuba and the United States: A Chronological History*. New York: Ocean, 1997, p. 11.

3. Quoted in *The Age of McCarthyism: A Brief History with Documents* (book review). www.bedfordstmartins.com/usingseries/hovey/schrecker%20.htm.

4. Quoted in Franklin, *Cuba and the United States*, p. 26.

5. Jason Berry, "The Bay of Pigs Invasion," *Exploring the Culture of Little Havana*. www.education.miami.edu/ep/LittleHavana/Monuments/Virgin1/The_Virgin_Mary/Bay_of_Pigs/bay_of_pigs.html.

6. Quoted in Franklin, *Cuba and the United States*, p. 36.

7. Mark J. White, *The Cuban Missile Crisis*. London: Macmillan, 1996, p. 35.

8. McGeorge Bundy, "Memorandum from the President's Special Assistant for National Security Affairs to President Kennedy," February 8, 1961.

9. Arthur Schlesinger Jr., "Memorandum from the President's Special Assistant to President Kennedy," February 11, 1961.

10. Quoted in National Security Archive, "Bay of Pigs: Forty Years After." www.gwu.edu/~nsarchive/bayofpigs/chron.html.

11. Quoted in Linda Robinson, "The Price of Military Folly," *U.S. News & World Report*, April 22, 1996, p. 2.

12. USS *Essex* Association, "Bay of Pigs History," November 30, 2002. www.ussessexcv9.org/Bay_Of_Pigs.htm.

13. Quoted in White, *The Cuban Missile Crisis*, p. 37.

14. Victor Andres Triay, *Bay of Pigs: An Oral History of Brigade 2506*. Gainesville: University Press of Florida, 2001, p. ix.

15. *Columbus Dispatch*, "Farewell, Havana," May 13, 2003. http://libpub.dispatch.com/cgi-bin/searchvl.

16. USA Engage, "USA Engage Calls for End to Cuban Travel Ban," April 23, 2003. www.usaengage.org/press_releases/2003/apr/cubatravel.htm.

Chapter 1

The Roots of the Invasion

1

Castro's Agenda Prompted the Formation of the Anti-Castro Militia

Victor Andres Triay

Victor Andres Triay is an associate professor of history at Middlesex Community College in Connecticut and the author of a number of works on the social history of Cuba. The following selection is from the introduction to his oral history of Brigade 2506, the anti-Castro militia that had been trained by the Central Intelligence Agency (CIA). Triay begins with the early history of the Cuban revolution, in which Fidel Castro, a radical student and lawyer, assumed control of the Cuban government while asserting that he was not a Communist. Later, Triay notes, it became obvious in Castro's actions and words that he indeed was pursuing a Communist agenda. Shortly after, he established a police state in which freedoms were revoked and opponents were executed. Drawing on the anti-American grumbling rippling through the country, Castro created a following based on hatred of the United States and its capitalist agenda. Punishments were strict for Castro's opponents, whose main goal was removing Castro and communism from their homeland. As tensions intensified, large numbers of Cubans fled to nearby Miami, Florida. Among these refugees were the founding members of Brigade 2506, who would later fight against Castro's forces in the Bay of Pigs invasion. These men were committed to liberating their home country and its people from Castro's tyrannical Communist rule.

Victor Andres Triay, *Bay of Pigs: An Oral History of Brigade 2506*. Gainesville: University Press of Florida, 2001. Copyright © 2001 by the Board of Regents of the State of Florida. All Rights Reserved. Reproduced by permission of the author.

The Caribbean nation of Cuba entered 1959 in a state of relief, hope, and festivity. Fulgencio Batista, the former military man and president who had disrupted the constitutional order when he launched his successful coup d'état in March 1952 and subsequently established a political dictatorship, had fled the country on New Year's Eve. Numerous groups, ranging from Cuba's democratic political parties to student organizations, had played a major role in his ouster. Of all the groups, however, the 26th of July Movement was the largest and most popular. Led by Fidel Castro, a dynamic former student radical and lawyer, the 26th of July had launched a campaign that included guerrilla warfare and urban sabotage. Castro and his rebels, wearing their trademark beards and military fatigues, arrived in Havana in early January and assumed control.

Cuba had achieved a relatively high standard of living by 1959. It consistently ranked at or near the top among American nations in all standard-of-living indicators. It had a large middle class, which comprised one-fourth to one-third of the population. Cuba's tight economic ties to the United States translated into equally strong cultural ones. Yet the political corruption that had become commonplace in Cuba caused a deep sense of frustration among many in the population. It was commonly believed that the country had not yet reached its social and economic potential because of its political difficulties. The level of poverty—especially in the countryside and certain parts of the cities—was viewed likewise as a major problem, as was the gap between black and white. The revolution, in large measure composed of people from the professional and middle classes and supported by all classes, promised to remedy the island's woes. A number of leaders who shared power with the 26th of July in Castro's early governments held democratic, liberal principles; many of them had fought dictatorship in Cuba even before Batista.

Castro's Intentions Are Revealed

Fidel Castro's true intentions, however, started to become clear as early as 1959. Whether he was a genuine Communist or a political opportunist is an open question, but even before Batista's ouster the 26th of July Movement had started cooperating with the island's Communist Party—although the Communists earlier had dismissed Castro's movement. Ernesto "Ché" Guevara and Raul Castro, Fidel's brother, had close contacts with the Communists and may have been responsible for the early ties. Whatever the circumstances, both supporters and opponents of the revolution began taking notice of the large number of Communists assigned to powerful, high-level positions within the first few months after Castro took over. A number of Cubans, including revolutionaries, condemned this. As the trend continued, people whose reformist ideals included an adherence to constitutional democracy turned against Castro, and many entered the opposition. . . .

By 1960, it became clear the Castro regime was not going to fulfill the promises of the revolution.

By 1960, it became clear the Castro regime was not going to fulfill the promises of the revolution. Instead it launched what amounted to a second revolution: the establishment of a totalitarian Communist police state personified by Fidel Castro. In the months to come, freedom of the press was destroyed, non-Castro political movements were brutally suppressed, and the right to a writ of habeas corpus (reinstated at one point by the revolution) was withdrawn. Also shut down or revolutionized were Cuba's universities, professional organizations, and labor unions. By mid-1960, all of the liberal ministers had been purged from the cabinet, and a number of foreign and domestic businesses had been seized. The promised elections were replaced by an "*¿Elecciones para qué?*" [Elections, what for?] campaign. The regime's take over of Cuba's entire institutional structure would make the imposition of a totalitarian state all the easier in the years to come. Neither Batista nor any other dictator in the region had ever established such complete control. Meanwhile, political prisons were being packed with thousands of real and imagined opponents, and executions had become part of the daily political landscape.

Castro's public anti-American rhetoric also had increased. In February 1960, a visit to Cuba by Soviet Deputy Premier Anastas Mikoyan prompted protests from students opposed to Communism. The economic arrangements made with the Soviet Union now made it clear to students and nonstudents alike that the Castro government was guiding Cuba into the Soviet camp. There were also threats to shut down Cuba's public and private schools and to replace them with schools that fostered the values of the new regime. This ultimately occurred in 1961. By then, the government had created highly regimented and Communist doctrine–oriented youth groups as well as similar militarized mass organizations that the public was expected to join. The regime also launched an antireligious campaign on the island and soon thereafter deported thousands of priests, nuns, ministers, and other clergy. Another campaign was begun to discredit the island's middle and upper classes in an effort to ignite class warfare.

The adoration much of the population had for Castro and his seemingly hypnotic hold over a large enough sector of the population gave him the backing he needed to carry out his programs. (Whether his backers truly constituted an electoral majority at any point shall never be known, as his rule was never validated through a democratic election.) In addition to his own inner circle and bureaucratic puppets, Castro's frontline fighters included the Committees for the Defense of the Revolution (the regime's neighborhood watchdog groups), an armed militia, the G.2 (secret police), revolutionary mobs, and the rebel army.

In Cuba, life had become impossible for Castro opponents.

A number of groups sprang up to oppose the regime's attempt to make Cuba a Communist nation. Among their ranks were many individuals who had been part of the revolution or, like most of the country, had at least been sympathetic to its initially stated aims. Many of them had participated in Batista's overthrow and had organized against Castro because they were horrified by what they saw as a betrayal of the revolution. The variety grew each day and included small and large university-based organizations, groups tied to the old democratic political parties, associations that included former Castro supporters, and numerous others. Catholic Church-oriented groups, strong early supporters of the revolution, also became active against Castro. Perhaps the greatest threat to Castro during this period was the guerrilla war that had been launched against him in the Escambray Mountains.

America Grows Wary of Castro

The U.S. government had also grown wary of Castro. At first it had supported the revolution by cutting off Batista militarily in 1958 and later by granting quick recognition to the new government. Nevertheless, it was not long before it became clear that Castro was no friend to the United States, as evidenced by his hostile rhetoric and, later, the seizure of American property. Furthermore, that he would create a Soviet base only ninety miles from U.S. shores was unacceptable and represented a genuine threat to national security. As Castro strengthened his hold over Cuba, it also became obvious that he was keen on casting the United States in the role of the villain. Not only would following such a course of action endear Castro to the Soviet Union, but a U.S. threat to the revolution would give him justification for his aggression against the domestic opposition as well as his other repressive social measures. Suspicious bombing raids launched from Florida, undoubtedly by his opponents and likely supported by the CIA, only gave him more ammunition in the propaganda war. In fact, the raids were so effective in strengthening the resolve of his loyalists and demonizing the United States that it appears the regime itself organized some of the flights.

The United States nevertheless sought a rapprochement with Castro in January 1960, using the Argentine ambassador as an intermediary. At the same time, the White House allowed the CIA to prepare a contingency plan aimed at ousting Castro. Although the first rapprochement effort failed, another attempt was made in March through the last liberal minister on Castro's cabinet, Finance Minister Rufo López Fresquet. It was rejected by Castro, and López Fresquet resigned. On the same day, [U.S. president Dwight] Eisenhower approved the CIA's plan. Still searching for a nonmilitary solution, however, the president suspended Cuba's sugar quota in July 1960, in an attempt to pressure Castro. This act often has been identified as one of the most pivotal events that helped drive Castro into the Soviet camp. However, the die had been cast: Castro's intention of making Cuba a Communist state aligned to the Soviet Union, as evidenced by his actions, was clear to many in

Cuba and the United States long before the cut in the sugar quota was even contemplated. Historian and [John F.] Kennedy advisor Arthur Schlesinger did not subscribe to the idea that the United States somehow pushed Castro into the arms of Moscow: "It was not until July 1960, long after Castro had effected the substantial communization of the government, army, and labor movement and had negotiated economic agreements with Russia and China, that the United States took public retaliatory action of a major sort. The suspension of the balance of Cuba's 1960 sugar quota (that same quota which Guevara had already denounced in March as 'economic slavery') was the conclusion, and not the cause, of Castro's hostility." In January 1961, the United States broke off diplomatic relations with Cuba.

Cubans Flee to Miami

In Cuba, life had become impossible for Castro opponents. The very act of organizing a dissenting political organization was unlawful, and being caught meant facing a very real threat of imprisonment or execution. Because there were no legal, constitutional outlets for the opposition, any group pitting itself against Castro had to do so clandestinely and at great risk. As the regime increased its control over the population and launched effective counterintelligence efforts, any likelihood that such groups would succeed diminished. As a result, many Castro opponents went overseas to continue the fight from abroad. The majority found themselves in neighboring Miami, Florida.

At the same time, large numbers of Cuban refugees began arriving in Miami. Unlike the relatively small wave in early 1959, this group was fleeing not because of Batista's ouster but because of Castro's imposition of a Marxist state. The composition of the Cuban exile community was severely altered, it now consisted overwhelmingly of people with no ties to the former dictator. A disproportionate number were part of Cuba's educated middle and upper classes. Among the exiled political leaders who arrived in Miami in late 1959 and 1960 were men who had been opponents of Batista and later, after his true motives were revealed, Fidel Castro. A number of them were well-known statesmen who had left organizations in Cuba that were secretly conspiring against the government. In 1960 the U.S. government entered into a partnership with a coalition created from those leaders, who were later organized as the provisional Cuban government that was to be landed in Cuba and recognized by the United States.

The Formation of Brigade 2506

An exile army, made up largely of young idealistic men from the exile community, likewise was assembled. Its objective ultimately became to seize and protect a beachhead from which the provisional democratic government could operate. The overall goal was to overthrow Castro and to reinstate the popular, progressive, and democratic constitution of 1940. The exile army was mostly recruited in Miami, trained in Central America, and landed on April 17, 1961, in the Bay of Pigs area on Cuba's southern shore. The small force, which took the name Brigade 2506 was a diverse group comprising all sectors of Cuban society. Students, workers, former Castro supporters, former army personnel, professionals, the rich, the poor, and the middle class all came together with the single unifying goal of ridding Cuba of Communist rule. Due in large part to decisions made in Washington shortly before the invasion, the Brigade was routed, captured, and imprisoned by Castro forces.

The invasion was nevertheless pivotal for the history of Cuba and its people, as it helped Fidel Castro consolidate his power and marked the true beginning of Communist rule on the island. And, as a result of the invasion's failure, the United States was faced not only with a Soviet base in the Caribbean but with over four decades of having Cuban refugees arrive on its shores. Among the approximately two million people in the Cuban exile community in the United States, the small group of men who made up Brigade 2506—although largely ignored by Americans—have always enjoyed the highest levels of respect and reverence.

2

U.S. Economic and Terrorist Acts Against Cuba Are Unwarranted

Fidel Castro

Just four days after Cuba's victory at the Bay of Pigs, Fidel Castro, president of the Council of State and the Council of Ministers of the Cuban government and the first secretary of the Communist Party of Cuba, gave a speech broadcast live on all Cuban television and radio stations. In the speech he announced the defeat of Brigade 2506, the CIA-trained anti-Castro militia. In the following excerpt from that speech, Castro describes with great passion the events leading up to the invasion. He condemns the United States for taking away most of Cuba's economic support, including its oil, sugar, and molasses markets, and then sending "terrorists" and "saboteurs" to destroy its factories and stores. Further, Castro argues that the United States tried to disable Cuba economically in the hopes of ousting him and taking control of the country's resources. Castro reminds his listeners that, to combat these U.S. actions, he brought about economic reforms that limited access to Cuban resources to wealthy Americans and extended those resources to Cuban workers. By using a vast array of examples, Castro encourages the people of Cuba to continue fighting attempts by the U.S. government to overtake their country and its resources. He cites the Bay of Pigs victory as proof that it can be done.

Fidel Castro, "Report to the Cuban People on the Victory at Playa Girón," *Playa Girón/Bay of Pigs: Washington's First Military Defeat in the Americas, April 23, 1961*, edited by Steve Clark and Mary-Alice Waters. New York: Pathfinder Press, 2001. Copyright © 2001 by Pathfinder Press. Reproduced by permission.

The public has been furnished with a large quantity of data on the invasion and its organization, as well as how it was crushed.

We will now make some general comments, as well as provide a more detailed account of how the enemy's whole plan developed. We will also review the revolution's plan and how it unfolded within the zone of operations.

In the first place, it had been known for some time, for almost a year, that an expeditionary force was being organized to attack our country. Ever since the triumph of the revolution, we have been living under threats, dangers, and perils. In other words, the revolution has had to constantly confront a series of possible attacks.

There were many different approaches on the part of the revolution's enemies, that is to say, on the part of imperialism, which is the only enemy with the strength and capacity to organize this type of attack. We always had to foresee different possibilities of action by imperialism against the revolution. One of these was some sort of indirect aggression—which is what they finally carried out, although it wasn't so indirect. It was indirect only in the sense of the individuals who personally participated in the invasion. It was a direct aggression insofar as these individuals were obeying orders from, and had received training in camps organized by the North Americans, using naval and airborne equipment furnished by the North Americans. The invading convoy was even escorted by U.S. Navy units; and even more, it had the direct aid and participation of the U.S. Air Force at one point. This is quite important.

That is why this was not your typical indirect aggression. It was rather a mixture of indirect and direct aggression. In other words, it was a mixed affair; not a direct aggression carried out by U.S. marines, their planes, and their military forces; neither was it a purely indirect aggression lacking participation by their military units. This means that they organized the invasion force primarily on the basis of using mercenaries, while they supported the invasion very directly with their navy and air force. . . .

Other Governments Resist U.S. Aggression

[The U.S. government] began preparations for indirect action right away, of course. It also maneuvered to organize some type of collective action against Cuba, which did not get very far. It did not get very far largely because of public opinion in Latin America favorable to the Cuban Revolution. This support has been and will increasingly become an insurmountable barrier to the U.S. government. It has forced certain hesitating governments in Latin America to maintain a firm stance against the U.S. moves, together with other Latin American governments that have held a firm stance all along. In this sense, the Mexican government has steadfastly opposed intervention in Cuba. The same is true of the regime of [Brazilian president Jânio] Quadros and the government of Ecuador.

In a word, the United States has encountered powerful resistance on the part of the governments and the peoples of Latin America in their attempt to organize an aggression with the help of the Organization of American States.

The United States Forms Corrupt Partnerships

Who could they rely on? Well, the United States has had to maneuver with the most corrupt, most discredited regimes in Latin America. At first they began by conniving with [Dominican Republic dictator Rafael Leónidas] Trujillo, and for a time the organization of aggression against Cuba seemed to be originating in Santo Domingo [capital of the Dominican Republic]. Subsequently, with the hypocrisy characteristic of an imperialist government, they began a new maneuver to enlist the support of a certain type of government in Latin America, the so-called representative democracies, in order to find a fig leaf to conceal their filthy policy. They then began to present themselves as enemies of Trujillo, inclining more toward a specific group of Latin American rulers who were not as discredited as Trujillo. . . .

In the end, the U.S. government was isolated in its plans of aggression against Cuba. It remained linked and associated with the governments of Guatemala and Nicaragua, which are the two governments most typically corrupt and despotic, and are reactionary enemies of the interests of the workers and peasants of those countries. These are the instruments Washington has been able to count on. The United States could not count on a government like Mexico's for a maneuver of this type, nor could it count on the government of Brazil. In short, it could not even count on other Latin American governments that were not willing to go so far in connection with U.S. moves against Cuba.

In other words, the U.S. partners in this adventure to bring about indirect aggression have been the most reactionary and most corrupt governments of Latin America, primarily the governments of Guatemala and Nicaragua.

Cuba Prepares for a Direct Attack

On certain occasions we have been under the threat of a direct attack, too. That threat has always been hanging over our heads, and more than once this idea picked up steam within U.S. ruling circles. One of those moments, during which we seemed to be on the verge of that type of direct aggression, was late last December [1960] and early January, that is, in the closing days of the [Dwight] Eisenhower administration.

We have been speaking out at the United Nations and everywhere else against the possibility of such an aggression, against the possibility that they might look for a pretext, that they might organize or prepare a "self-aggression," something the United States has done under various circumstances every time they have wanted to carry out a plan of military aggression. They have always managed to invent or fabricate a pretext. . . . We have always followed a very cautious policy to avoid giving the United States a pretext to attack our country. . . .

Our frame of mind as to the possibility of a direct aggression has always been perfectly clear: we are determined to resist to the last man! That is our determination. Naturally, however, we are interested in avoiding that aggression. No nation can remain indifferent to the destruction of resources and lives such an event would entail. Hence our interest in avoiding that type of aggression. That is why we have made every possible effort to keep them from having the slightest pretext. We have always been alerting the world as to our position in this respect, so as to make it as difficult as possible for them to take a step of that nature. . . .

The Need for Economic Independence

Prior to the revolution our economy was based around exports to a single market, and on the production of a single item: sugar. Our economy was based on the cultivation of a single crop. It was based on the export of that crop to a single market, the U.S. market. Our economy was completely dependent on the United States.

That is why the watchword of economic independence has been repeated so often in our country. And that's why nearly everybody kept repeating the slogan that "there is no political independence without economic independence." That was simply a fact recognized by everyone. We did not have economic independence. Why not? Because we were entirely dependent, above all on the U.S. market. In addition, our imports came almost exclusively from the United States.

Our frame of mind as to the possibility of a direct aggression has always been perfectly clear: we are determined to resist to the last man!

Moreover, our country's economy was also in the hands of U.S. monopolies. The banks, the main industries, the mines, the fuel, the electric power, the telephones, a large portion of our best arable lands, the most important sugar mills—all these belonged to U.S. monopolies. Our economy was totally dependent on the United States. That's why we could not call ourselves a truly free country, because we were not economically free.

That was the situation when the revolution came to power. It immediately began to introduce a series of reforms and revolutionary laws designed to transform the country's economic structure. These revolutionary laws brought about an immediate clash with the monopolistic interests in the United States. And a clash with the monopolistic interests in the United States means a clash with the ruling circles in the United States. Because when all is said and done, in the United States the monopolies and the government are one and the same thing. . . .

Castro Expels the U.S. Military Mission

In our country, when a series of social and economic reforms began to be enacted, we too clashed with U.S. interests. In this case, however, the imperialists did not have—as they had in other countries, such as Guatemala—a professional army trained and led by their embassies that could be utilized against the people's government. In Cuba the professional army had been destroyed, the old army was destroyed, and the weapons were totally in the hands of the peasants and the workers, who were the ones that made up the ranks of the Rebel Army. The weapons were in the hands of the people.

The U.S. Military Mission had been operating in Cuba until the very day of Batista's fall. . . .

We told them, . . . "Well, the best thing you can do is go home as soon as possible, because we don't need you.". . .

So there was no more Military Mission. They no longer had an instrument here to use for establishing relations with the military high command who could be utilized in face of some political conjuncture. The situation they found themselves in here in Cuba was a bit more complicated. It was not the same as in Guatemala, because they could not rely on a professional army, or on a Military Mission. Instead they had to deal with an entirely new army, led by men who had been in the war and were in no way connected with them. In fact, it was commanded by men whose class interests were diametrically opposed to those defended by the former professional army.

In other words, they could not count on an army in Cuba to carry out a coup d'état. The government had enormous popular support. The revolutionary government had a brand new army whose members came from the ranks of the people. So what could they do? . . .

Cuba Enacts Economic Reform

That's when the economic aggression, the plans of harassment began. . . . They carried out that aggression against a country that was, first of all, an underdeveloped country. Secondly, a country that was accustomed to a number of luxury items and imports that in recent years had exceeded our exports. So one of the first things the revolutionary government did was to adopt a policy of austerity, of frugality. It was not a policy of austerity at the expense of the workers or peasants, because the peasants were not the ones who drove Cadillacs, the peasants and the workers were not the people who took trips to Paris or the United States. The peasants and the workers were not the ones who consumed those luxury items. But the country as a whole was spending—I believe the imports of automobiles alone amounted to about $30 million a year. And the spare parts for these cars amounted to a fantastic sum, too. Meanwhile, only about $5 million a year was spent on agricultural implements. . . .

Tens and hundreds of thousands of families were without work, going hungry, totally dependent on the sugar harvest, which gave them three months of work—three months that in general were devoted to paying off the debts they had incurred during the "dead season.". . .

So the revolution adopted, to start with, a set of policies in the interests of the people. It lowered rents, it cut public utility rates, it gave idle lands to the cooperatives, it developed agriculture. It invested tremendous resources in farm implements, to give employment to everybody. It initiated a policy that, on the one hand, greatly benefited the people, and on the other hand, restricted the import of luxury items so those funds could be used not to purchase luxury cars but to buy farm implements and industrial machinery.

Tens and hundreds of thousands of families were without work, going hungry, totally dependent on the sugar harvest.

Thus, by means of that policy of frugality, the government was achieving an extraordinary rise in our foreign exchange reserves. That was just the opposite of what the imperialists thought would happen. When they speak to Latin America of an austerity policy, they are referring to an austerity policy that sacrifices the people, sacrifices the workers and peasants, that freezes wages, and a whole series of measures that don't affect in the least the standard of living, the spending, the tastes, or the income of the economically dominant classes, to whom that sort of austerity policy never entailed any sacrifice. We, on the other hand, adopted an austerity policy that affected the social classes that were precisely the ones who spent the most on luxuries, on expensive items and trips. In other words, we refused to turn over all the dollars requested by those ladies and gentlemen for travel expenses; we gave them a limited amount. In the old days they used to take their Cuban pesos to the bank and ask for $10,000 for trips to Paris. But when the revolution triumphed, things changed. We said: you can have a greatly reduced number of dollars for trips to Paris.

An austerity policy was established that did not affect the people, it affected the dominant economic classes only. That policy was designed precisely to obtain agricultural equipment, to build factories, to raise educational levels, and to improve housing and health conditions for those classes that work for a living. . . .

The revolution [in other words] established an austerity policy that benefited the workers and peasants, while calling for sacrifices by the economically dominant classes. . . .

The Battle for Oil

Our foreign exchange reserves kept growing. At that point, as it dawned on [the United States] what was happening, they took another step of aggression: they began with oil.

Castro (center) during the insurgence against the Batista regime. Castro condemned the invasion at the Bay of Pigs and encouraged Cubans to fight against the U.S. government.

Everybody remembers how they attempted to leave us without oil.

Being very much interested in selling our products in other markets, we had signed an agreement to sell a certain quantity of sugar to the Soviet Union in exchange for buying oil from them. We were using our sugar to buy oil.

Before that happened, we had to pay for oil in dollars, acquiring it from countries that did not buy any of our sugar. Given the country's interest in saving foreign exchange so that it could be invested in industrial and agricultural machinery, it was to our benefit to sell sugar to other markets and receive in payment articles that previously had been paid for in dollars. So we sold sugar to the Soviet Union and purchased oil from them.

When we told the U.S. oil companies that a portion of our crude oil requirement was going to be acquired from the Soviet Union, they decided not to refine any Soviet petroleum here. They would not refine it unless the oil came from the wells controlled by them in other countries of the world. Such a setup brought them fabulous profits, because they controlled both the refineries and the extraction of oil in other countries. They are typical monopolies. They own the oil wells. They own the oil pipelines. They transport the oil through the pipelines. They refine the oil. And they handle distribution of the oil. That's a monopoly.

When they were told that part of the fuel we would be consuming was going to come from other sources, they refused to refine that oil. Why did they refuse? Because they thought, if Cuba takes any measures against us, then we'll leave them without oil; and if a country is left without oil, it will go through a tremendous crisis as a consequence of lack of fuel, and this would inflict a harsh blow to the revolution.

What we did was to take over those refineries. And the Soviet Union made a tremendous effort to supply us with all the oil we needed. This effort bore fruit, and we withstood that aggression, which would have left the country without oil—thanks to the effort by the Soviet Union to maintain the supply of oil, so that we have not lacked it up to today. Moreover, the oil is cheaper, much cheaper, than what we used to pay to the U.S. monopolies. Not to mention the fact that we don't pay for it in dollars, but in accordance with the trade agreements we have signed with other countries; that is, we pay for it with sugar. Moreover, while we buy oil, we sell other things; previously we bought oil but did not sell anything.

So we overcame that situation. They saw the revolution's success in confronting that aggression involving oil. At the same time, they saw our foreign exchange reserves keep going up, enabling us to forge ahead with our economic development plans. So they decided to take another step. What did it consist of? They canceled our sugar quota, that is, they shut us out of the U.S. market.

United States Bans Cuban Sugar Exports

It would have been extremely difficult for any government, under normal circumstances, to withstand that kind of blow. An aggression of that type can be withstood only by a revolutionary government, with the support of a revolutionary people. That aggression meant our country would be deprived of the hundreds of millions of dollars we received for our sugar in the U.S. market.

In the old days, when Cuba sold its sugar on the U.S. market, the most important sugar mills and the most productive sugarcane-producing lands were owned by U.S. interests. In other words the trade was really trade among themselves. They grew the cane, which was then harvested by our workers for a miserable wage, working only part of the year at that; the cane was processed at U.S.-owned sugar mills; and the sugar was sold to the U.S. market.

Consequently, there was no profit for our country. Who got the profits? The oil monopolies, the public utility monopolies, the sugar monopolies.

"Let's see how you get along. Either you surrender or we ruin you. We'll blockade you through hunger."

When the country carried out the agrarian reform, we organized cooperatives to give employment to those peasants on a year-round basis and to have them diversify their production. Not only would they grow sugarcane, but all types of foodstuffs they needed. Just at that moment, when our people were beginning to receive the benefits of the work in the fields and in the factories, they deprived us of the U.S. market, and they deprived our country of hundreds of millions of dollars it used to receive.

What was the aim? To make the revolution submit, to force the people down on their knees, to make our people surrender. They said: "We are going to deprive you of that income. Let's see how you get along. Either you surrender or we ruin you. We'll blockade you through hunger." But our people reacted to that policy with the determination to press ahead.

In face of the imperialist aggression, once again the Soviet Union, together with the other socialist countries—despite the fact that they were heavy sugar producers and did not need all that sugar—made a great effort to acquire from us four million tons of sugar. They did this so our revolution could withstand the U.S. economic aggression. . . .

Once again the revolution, though at the expense of effort and sacrifice, was able to keep moving forward, despite the imperialist aggression.

The United States Bans Other Exports

What did they do then? They took further steps and prohibited all exports of raw materials and spare parts to our country. What did that mean? Simply that all the factories in Cuba, almost all of them, almost all the transportation system in Cuba, almost all the moving equipment—in the construction industry, in agriculture, in industry—in short, some 95 percent of the industrial equipment and machinery in our country used to come from the United States.

Many factories even used raw materials that were produced only in the United States. Not satisfied with taking away our market, they instituted a ban on those exports. Why? To leave us without raw materials or spare parts for all our transport industry, our construction industry, our agriculture, and our factories.

Some of those factories require thousands of different space parts, because they use a wide assortment of different types of parts that are extremely difficult to obtain in other markets. So they took a further step and stopped exports of those items.

As if that were not enough, they took still further steps. Now they were no longer just blocking our export of sugar, but also our exports of other products, such as sugarcane molasses, for instance. Our molasses had already been sold to its traditional market—U.S. market—because the law they had enacted there against Cuba did not say anything about molasses; so some U.S. companies had already purchased our molasses. And through pressures exerted by the State Department, they took away from our country the $15 million it was going to receive from the sale of molasses.

To sell molasses in other places is more difficult. Why? Because it requires special storage facilities and a certain type of ship to transport it. It is not easy to get a sufficient number of such vessels.

U.S. Attempts to Destroy Castro's Government

In short, what was involved was one step after another designed to blockade us, drive us to shortages, to a difficult economic situation.

Why did they do this? Simply to defeat the revolutionary government, which was enacting laws in the interest of the working people. They wanted to bring back to our country government by the bootleggers, the gamblers, the racketeers, the embezzlers, governments that served the interests of the electric company and the telephone company. They wanted to bring back governments that, whenever the telephone company might want a new, more advantageous, contract, raising rates by a nickel for each additional call, would say, "Yes sir!" A government that, when the mining companies wanted concessions, would say, "Yes sir!" A government that, faced with any request for concessions in our markets, in transportation, or anywhere else, would say, "Yes sir!" They wanted a government, in short, that would hand over our country's economy and our people's interests to the monopolies.

> *They organized sabotage raids against our sugar mills, against our wealth, they organized the burning of our canefields.*

They wanted to replace the revolutionary government with a government of crooks, swindlers, embezzlers, and murderers. They wanted a government of ignorance. They wanted to overthrow a government that sends teachers to the remotest corners of the country, that creates jobs for hundreds of thousands of peasants without work, that increases the number of construction workers from 30,000 to nearly 90,000—in short, a government that stands up to the aggression. Because the revolution's merit is that all the work being done is occurring in the midst of one aggression after another. First with oil refineries; next, the sugar quota; then the blockade barring all exports of raw materials and spare parts, followed by the blockade of all other products.

Yet imperialism is not satisfied with taking away our sugar quota and blocking our sales to the United States. They also pressure other countries they have influence over to prevent us from selling to them. And while all these attacks are going on, the revolution is building houses, developing cooperatives, raising agricultural production, constructing beach facilities, carrying out reforestation plans, engaging in an educational campaign throughout the country. This gives an idea of what this country could have done had they not taken away our sugar quota, had they not attacked us economically.

Counterrevolutionaries Organize

But that was not enough. Cuba kept resisting. So they started to organize terrorists and saboteurs, who were specially trained in the United States to become experts in handling inflammable materials and explosives. They began a campaign of destruction against our stores and factories.

There was the case of the electric power company, which never had any trouble when it belonged to a U.S. monopoly. After it became the property of the people, its rates were cut and its earnings no longer wound up in the coffers of U.S. banks. At that point a campaign of sabotage was launched against it.

The El Encanto department store used to be for the rich, and its profits benefited some rich man and no one else. Back then that store had no problems. But as soon as the big industries became the property of the people, the Yankee Central Intelligence Agency . . . began campaigns of sabotage to destroy our industrial plants, our factories, and our sugar production.

The Hershey Sugar Mill was never set on fire when it belonged to Mr. [Julio] Lobo, who had, I believe, fourteen sugar mills and fifteen thousand caballerías of land [some half million acres]. But that changed when that same sugar mill became the property of the nation, when Lobo's lands became the property of the people's cooperatives—you should see how different the peasant's life is there now; you should see how the peasant lives in those cooperatives, compared to how he lived in the past. So they come to destroy that wealth, which they would never have thought of destroying before, when it belonged to a gentleman who owned fourteen sugar mills. They come to destroy it now that those lands belong to twelve or fourteen thousand families, who are the cooperative members working those lands.

It seems that for imperialism—that gang of sanctimonious liars and hypocrites—what's fair is for one man to own fourteen thousand caballerías of land, while fifteen or twenty thousand families go hungry. What's unfair, for them, is for the former owner not to own land. What's unfair, for them, is for 15,000 families to have land, a house, a job, food, and a school all year round. According to the imperialist gringo mentality, the imperialist conception of justice, one thing is fair and the other thing is unfair.

So they organized sabotage raids against our sugar mills, against our wealth, they organized the burning of our canefields. As you will recall, they began with planes that came openly from U.S. territory, though in the end such activities created such a scandal that they changed their tactics and methods for setting our canefields on fire.

But that was not enough for them. They began to organize groups of counterrevolutionaries, for which they recruited former military men, deserters, lumpens, the worst types. And the very worst were those who commanded the so-called Second Front of the Escambray, whose history is well known to you all. Utilizing all those elements, they organized groups of counterrevolutionaries at the service of imperialism, and sent more and more weapons. . . .

So our country has been subjected to a continuous and systematic campaign of harassment and aggression. These include economic attacks, such as the moves against our oil and our sugar. They include the halting of exports from the United States, in order to leave us without spare parts and raw materials, the blockade of other Cuban exports not only to the United States, but to other countries as well. There were also the sabotage campaigns and the organization of groups of counterrevolutionary guerrillas.

3

The United States Should Not Carry Out the Bay of Pigs Plan

Chester Bowles

In this memo originally sent to Secretary of State Dean Rusk and then forwarded to President John F. Kennedy, Under Secretary of State Chester Bowles argues against the Bay of Pigs invasion. Written on March 31, 1961, a little over two weeks before the invasion, the memo outlines four major problems with the plan. First, Bowles argues that by carrying out the invasion, the United States would violate the Act of Bogota, which prohibits the involvement of a state or group of states with the affairs of any other state. Bowles's second point is that the plan has a high risk of failure, and such failure will only make Cuban leader Fidel Castro stronger. As well, the plan will increase anti-American sentiment throughout the world. Furthermore, if this plan appears to be failing in its early stages, then the United States will likely be drawn into direct involvement. By taking direct action against Cuba, the U.S. government risks losing its reputation as a fair and impartial world leader. Finally, Bowles argues that even though the United States has spent a great deal of time and money planning for this invasion, it should not feel compelled to proceed if there are any reservations whatsoever.

O n Tuesday, April 4th [1961,] a meeting will be held at the White House at which a decision will be reached on the Cuban adventure. . . .

Chester Bowles, "Memorandum from Under Secretary of State Chester Bowles to Secretary of State Dean Rusk," March 31, 1961.

I have had an opportunity to become better acquainted with the proposal, and I find it profoundly disturbing.

Let me frankly say, however, that I am not a wholly objective judge of the practical aspects.

In considerable degree, my concern stems from a deep personal conviction that our national interests are poorly served by a covert operation of this kind at a time when our new President [John F. Kennedy] is effectively appealing to world opinion on the basis of high principle.

I have had the opportunity to become better acquainted with the proposal, and I find it profoundly disturbing.

Even in our imperfect world, the differences which distinguish us from the Russians are of vital importance. This is true not only in a moral sense but in the practical effect of these differences on our capacity to rally the non-Communist world in behalf of our traditional democratic objectives.

In saying this, I do not overlook the ruthless nature of the struggle in which we are involved, nor do I ignore the need on occasion for action which is expedient and distasteful. Yet I cannot persuade myself that means can be *wholly* divorced from ends—even within the context of the Cold War.

Against this background, let me suggest several points which I earnestly hope will be fully taken into account in reaching the final decision.

Violating the Act of Bogota

1. In sponsoring the Cuban operation, for instance, we would be deliberately violating the fundamental obligations we assumed in the Act of Bogota establishing the Organization of American States (OAS). The Act provides:

"No State or group of States has the right to intervene, directly or indirectly, for any reason whatever, in the internal or external affairs of any other State. The foregoing principle prohibits not only armed force but also any other form of interference or attempted threat against the personality of the State or against its political, economic and cultural elements.

"No State may use or encourage the use of coercive measures of an economic or political character in order to force the sovereign will of another State and obtain from it advantages of any kind.

"The territory of a State is inviolable; it may not be the object, even temporarily, of military occupation or of other measures of force taken by another State, directly or indirectly, on any grounds whatever. . . ."

I think it fair to say that these articles, signalling an end of U.S. unilateralism, comprise the central features of the OAS from the point of view of the Latin American countries.

To act deliberately in defiance of these obligations would deal a blow to the Inter-American System from which I doubt it would soon recover. The suggestion that Cuba has somehow "removed itself" from the System is a transparent rationalization for the exercise of our own will.

More generally, the United States is the leading force in and substantial beneficiary of a network of treaties and alliances stretching around the world. That these treaty obligations should be recognized as binding in law and conscience is the condition not only of a lawful and orderly world, but of the mobilization of our own power.

We cannot expect the benefits of this regime of treaties if we are unwilling to accept the limitations it imposes upon our freedom to act.

A Low Chance of Success

2. Those most familiar with the Cuban operation seem to agree that as the venture is now planned, the chances of success are not greater than one out of three. This makes it a highly risky operation. If it fails, Castro's prestige and strength will be greatly enhanced.

The one way we can reduce the risk is by a sharply increased commitment of direct American support. In talking to Bob McNamara and Ros Gilpatric . . . at the Pentagon, I gathered that this is precisely what the military people feel we should do.

The U.S. Reputation Will Be Compromised

3. Under the very best of circumstances, I believe this operation will have a much more adverse effect on world opinion than most people contemplate. It is admitted that there will be riots and a new wave of anti-Americanism throughout Latin America. It is also assumed that there will be many who quietly wish us well and, if the operation suc-

ceeds, will heave a sigh of relief.

Moreover, even if the reaction in Latin America is less damaging than we expect, I believe that in Europe, Asia, and Africa, the reaction against the United States will be angry and the fresh, favorable image of the Kennedy Administration will be correspondingly dimmed. It would be a grave mistake for us to minimize this factor and its impact on our capacity to operate effectively in cooperation with other nations in other parts of the world.

Failure Will Jeopardize Our Favorable Position

4. If the operation appears to be a failure in its early stages, the pressure on us to scrap our self-imposed restriction on direct American involvement will be difficult to resist, and our own responsibility correspondingly increased. . . .

Since January 20th our position has been dramatically improved in the eyes of the world vis-à-vis the Soviet Union.

The Kennedy Administration has been doing particularly well in Africa and Latin America, and with a little luck in Laos and more affirmative policies, we may soon be able to improve our position in East Asia, South Asia, and the Middle East. Within the next few months we can also begin to strengthen our relations with Western Europe.

I believe it would be a grave mistake for us to jeopardize the favorable position we have steadily developed in most of the non-Communist world by the responsible and restrained policies which are now associated with the President by embarking on a major covert adventure with such very heavy built-in risks.

I realize that this operation has been put together over a period of months. A great deal of time and money has been put into it, and many able and dedicated people have become emotionally involved in its success. We should not, however, proceed with this adventure simply because we are wound up and cannot stop.

Chapter 2

The Invasion Fails

1

The U.S. Betrayal of the Cuban Militia Caused Heavy Losses

Manuel Penabaz

Manuel Penabaz was a member of Brigade 2506, the CIA-trained militia that stormed the beaches of the Bay of Pigs in Cuba on April 17, 1961. Penabaz was one of the lucky few who escaped capture that day. A year and a half later, his story of the invasion was published in the *U.S. News & World Report*, revealing an inside view of the events of the failed strike against Cuban leader Fidel Castro. Penabaz discusses the ways in which antirevolutionaries were recruited and trained and the role of the U.S. military in planning and organizing the invasion. He provides a graphic account of the three days of fighting that ended in the capture or death of nearly all of his comrades. Penabaz attributes these massive losses to the lack of support from the U.S. government in terms of ammunition and air cover. He views the U.S. failure to provide support not only as the cause of the deaths of the Cuban refugees who perished in the invasion but also as a lost opportunity to defeat communism in Cuba and around the world.

"Keep advancing! Keep advancing—and wait!" So long as I live, I shall never forget those words. They sounded out from an American ship, from the officer who directed our landing operations at the Bay of Pigs on the coast of Cuba, where 1,500 of us Cubans offered our lives in

Manuel Penabaz, "'We Were Betrayed': A Veteran of the Cuban Invasion Speaks Out," *U.S. News & World Report*, January 14, 1963, pp. 46–49.

the hope of liberating our beloved country from the rule of the bearded despot, Fidel Castro, on April 17, 1961.

"Keep advancing and firing! Take the area ahead—and wait!"

To us who had struggled ashore from our landing barges, the words "and wait" meant only one thing: "Help is on the way."

When we were recruited for this perilous mission, and during our exhaustive training in Guatemala—even while on the slow, ancient freighters that brought us from our embarkation port in Nicaragua—we were promised the support of the armed forces of the United States.

"Over you will be air cover," we were told, "and back of you the Navy and land forces of the United States and other free nations of the Americas. You cannot fail."

We did not fail. We were betrayed.

After three days of fighting, we heard again that same American voice that had exhorted us to "keep advancing—and wait." Only this time it said:

"We cannot give you any further support."

The whole invasion operation that had been planned and directed by agencies of the U.S. Government had been abandoned by that Government at the moment when victory could have overthrown Fidel Castro.

Of the 1,500 who began the assault at the Bay of Pigs on that warm April morning, about 100 were killed; 60 later died of wounds, starvation, torture and executions; most of the others were captured.

I was among the lucky. I escaped. Four of my comrades and I found a raft and, after five days afloat, were rescued.

Now my surviving comrades of that invasion also have been freed—ransomed from Castro's prison cells. Many of them have told me since their arrival in Miami that their lips are sealed because they have relatives still in Cuba. I, too, have relatives in Cuba. But my lips are not sealed. I will tell the story of what happened at the Bay of Pigs, because I believe that such a mistake must not be made again by any government or people of the free world.

Recruiting Cuban Exiles

For me, the story of the invasion began in Miami, Fla., when I heard the words: "Recruits are needed—recruits to overthrow Castro."

The Central Intelligence Agency of the U.S. Government, headed by Allen Dulles, was the recruiting and training group for our volunteers.

Several officers of the Central Intelligence Agency were operating in the Miami area, seeking out the leaders among the Cuban exiles and encouraging them to select the likeliest young men for the adventure. I was told that there would be an invasion of Cuba "fairly early in 1961," backed and supported by the United States.

I was among the lucky. I escaped.

The first airlifts of volunteers to training camps began in late summer, 1960. Any recruits who doubted that the United States was back of the operation were assured that, when we reached our training camps, we would find American officers in charge and there would be the best of American weapons to carry into battle.

Sure enough, when we arrived at Trax Base, high in the mountains of Guatemala, American officers were in charge of the camp, and our weapons were among the best the U.S. had to offer.

At Retalhuleu, Guatemala, a splendid airstrip had been laid down by American engineers. All about were huge accumulations of war material—aircraft, mortars, tons of bombs and other ammunition.

Training Begins

Over the whole operation, there was an air of great secrecy. Our instructors, American officers, wore only fatigue uniforms, with no markings. We knew them only by first names. But it was apparent that they were experienced and efficient.

It did not take us long to learn that "Frank," the man who gave the orders for both Americans and Cubans, was a colonel. The American subordinate officers were all experts in their fields. "Ray" was our rifle and pistol instructor. It leaked out that he was from California and a pistol champion. "Sam," chief trainer of the parachutists, was plainly a veteran of many combat jumps. "Nick," from New Mexico, was our instructor for intelligence operations. "Bob" demonstrated all there was to know about mortars and machine guns. "Pat" was a security officer.

There was no secrecy about the CIA man in charge at the camp. He was Frank Bender, a man of German descent who had fought in the French underground during World War II. Bender was everywhere—shuttling back to Miami to check on recruiting, going to Washington and New York to try to bring all the Cuban exile leaders together into one united front.

Trax Base was a regular little city, built by the U.S. Government. It had modern paved streets, electric lights and barracks for about 500 men. As our numbers grew, we had to disperse to four other training bases.

All the training bases were leased from Roberto Alejo, brother of the Guatemalan Ambassador to the United States and a trusted friend of Guatemalan President Miguel Ydígoras Fuentes.

For rifles, we had that infantry workhorse, the M-1 Garand, firing eight shots. Officers carried carbines. We learned to use machine guns and bazookas, 57-millimeter guns and 4.2-inch mortars.

Training was rugged, but we endured it cheerfully.

One prized piece of equipment was an electronic communications-control center—a device so new that it had never been used in combat. It was manned by six men, who could relay messages to artillery, aircraft and other combat units. The American officers warned us that it should be destroyed rather than be permitted to fall into the hands of the enemy.

Training was rugged, but we endured it cheerfully. We were preparing to free our land of Marxist dictatorship. We understood that our brigade would be the initial attacking party backed by the might of the United States. There would be ample ammunition to stop Castro's tanks and his land forces. Every effort would be made to win the support of the Cuban people. Exile leaders would be formed into a provisional government and would receive the recognition of the U.S. and of Latin-American countries. Such were our assurances.

Our brigade commander, Col. José Perez San Roman, and his headquarters staff hoped that, before embarking, they could have printed thousands of leaflets to be dropped all over Cuba by planes calling upon the people to rise against their oppressor, Fidel Castro.

At the last moment San Roman was informed that the U.S. Government could not approve this plan.

The Troops Set Sail

On the morning of April 10 we were flown to Puerto Cabezas, Nicaragua. At the dock we saw the invasion "fleet" that the CIA had mobilized. There were six ancient craft. Three were Liberty ships of World War II vintage. The other three were old fishing yachts. Most of the officers were Spanish or Cuban, with crews filled out from men of the U.S. merchant marine—among them many drunkards and misfits. We soon discovered that the crews did not want to mix with their live Cuban cargoes, and couldn't have cared less whether the expedition succeeded or failed.

"We carry you, land you and leave you," a crew member explained. We took this as added assurance that we would be covered by air and naval support, for it was unthinkable to us that any civilized government would send men to battle without ample means either for complete victory or honorable retreat.

On the night of April 11, in moonless darkness, we sailed. On the fourth day at sea, we were given our final briefing on our invasion plan. Each man received a mimeographed copy of the operation in detail. The landings would be made on April 17 at Bahia de Cochinos; the Bay of Pigs, about 90 miles southeast of Havana. Battalions 2 and 5 would land first, at Playa Larga, deep in the bay, under command of Eneido Olivia. All other units would land at Playa Girón. Soon after our landings, the parachutists would drop some 12 miles inland to seize the airport of Jagüey Grande.

I looked back toward our ships. One was in flames and sinking rapidly.

On the morning of April 15, planes from the Nicaraguan bases would begin bombing Castro's airfields and hangars, to be followed by heavier strikes on the sixteenth and seventeenth. Some of our units would move southeastward to join rebel groups in the Escambray Mountains, and others

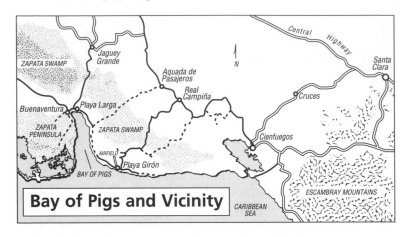

Bay of Pigs and Vicinity

would move westward to take Havana.

Most important of all, our leaders had been assured of U.S. air cover, the backing of the U.S. Navy and—if needed—of U.S. land troops as well. No one expected our 1,500 volunteers alone to conquer Castro's forces of 300,000 militia and regulars.

But we did expect that, with our American equipment plus American battle support, we would move inland steadily until we had cut Cuba in two. Castro's forces would then realize resistance was hopeless. Defections would begin and rise like a tide.

Bombs Are Dropped

Soon we heard the Cuban radio announcing angrily that several planes were bombing the airports of Santiago and Havana and various military bases. We were elated. The bombings by our planes from Nicaragua had gone off on schedule. But Castro's broadcast was followed by a rebroadcast from the United States that chilled us to the bone. It was a speech by President Kennedy in which he affirmed that the U.S. would maintain a policy of strict neutrality in Cuba's internal affairs. Specifically, said the President, his Government would not intervene in the events shaping up in that island.

"He must say that, to deceive Castro," we finally decided, for all of us had heard Mr. Kennedy, during his campaign for the Presidency, advocate full support of Cubans opposing Castro. Yet doubts assailed me. It was the President speaking now—not the candidate.

The Battle at Playa Larga

On the morning of the sixteenth we were heartened by the sight of two U.S. destroyers, one on either side of our slow-moving flotilla. They were greeted with cheers. At least, we thought, we would have naval support. And, in case of setback, we would be evacuated and saved from capture.

All through that April 16 we waited for news of the second bombing strike. No news came.

That night we saw the lights of Girón Beach, Bay of Pigs, on the horizon, like shimmering pearls. The ships carrying Oliva's units had veered to our right and his men would be landing soon. As the first shots from Playa Larga sounded, I looked at my watch. It was 20 minutes past midnight, April 17. The tragic invasion had begun.

Oliva and his two battalions met little resistance on their landings—only a small patrol of Castro's militia.

Our ships drew up about 1 kilometer—.6 of a mile—from the shore and anchored. Landing barges were quickly floated, and all hands began unloading the weapons.

The firing on Playa Larga had ceased. Back and forth from all the ships shuttled the motorized landing barges. As dawn broke, our radios picked up the first message of the American officer, stationed farther out at sea on a U.S. warship. He said:

"The whole bay is ours. The enemy has disappeared."

We learned later that morning that the officer was on the aircraft carrier *Boxer*. How comforting to know that the might of the greatest navy in the world was standing by to support this blow for freedom!

Our ship's captain stuck his head out of his cabin and shouted: "The sky is ours, too." Every man raised a cheer, for surely this meant that the bombing of the fifteenth had destroyed Castro's Air Force.

Landing at the Bay of Pigs

But we cheered too soon. At 6 A.M., a B-26 bomber flew toward us at low altitude. We supposed it came from our Nicaragua base. But suddenly it swooped low and began firing at the barges unloading their cargoes on the beach.

"Shoot!" I shouted to the men still on my ship, the *Atlantico*. There was also firing from other ships. The B-26 sped away. It had given our men their first baptism of fire. But, most important to Castro, the pilot had learned that there was no air cover for the landing.

Two other B-26s appeared from over the sea. Several of our guns started firing. Then the planes identified themselves as ours, from the Nicaragua base. They circled over our landings for a while. Then, with feelings of despair, we saw them head back toward Nicaragua. The pilots said they had fuel enough to cruise over the Bay of Pigs for only about 20 minutes.

Suddenly a Sea Fury appeared. I recognized this British-made fighter plane at once, for Dictator [Fulgencio] Batista had used them against us when I was fighting with Castro in the hills. This one made a pass or two, then zoomed away.

"We cannot give you any further support. You are on your own."

As our landing barge was on its way toward the beach, another Castro B-26 appeared, swooping directly over us. Our guns fired. The plane plunged into the sea.

We waded ashore, through the warm Cuban waters, onto the beach of our native land. Soon we were under terrific fire from several enemy aircraft. Flat on our bellies, many of us crawled into the village of Girón. Some of the inhabitants had fled. Many others ran toward us with welcoming shouts.

The Naval Fleet Is Attacked

I looked back toward our ships. One was in flames and sinking rapidly. It was the *Houston*—with most of its precious cargo still unloaded. The stacks of mortar shells, the armored trucks, the electronic communications-control center—all were going down! Another ship burst into flames. It was the *Rio Escondido*. Soon it, too, sank. All the other ships were moving rapidly away. We watched a Sea Fury bring down a B-26 from our base. We asked:

"When will our air cover come? When will those fast U.S. jets go into action?"

The news from Playa Larga was good. Oliva had moved inland, destroying seven enemy tanks and numerous trucks, along with hundreds of enemy soldiers. The news from the parachutists was less hopeful. They had dropped early in the morning, but, for the most part, had landed in the swampy terrain north of the bay. Now they were fighting their way back to join our main force. By midafternoon, we were moving steadily forward.

"Keep advancing! Move inland—and wait!" the American officer's voice kept broadcasting.

Castro's Tanks Advance

Late in the day we encountered the first battalions of Castro's militia, advancing among 10 or 12 tanks. How we needed those antitank mines that went down with the *Houston!* But our mortars were ready. We let go our barrage. Our fire was devastating. Castro's poor militiamen fell in heaps. Men? The majority were mere boys—many no more than 14 years of age. Only an insane sadist would have drafted those adolescents to fill his military machine.

As one after another of their tanks were knocked out, the Castro infantry ran like crazy from side to side. Our men got tired of shooting at them. The butchery that went on is impossible to describe. By nightfall, the survivors of Castro's forces were in full retreat. . . .

Hopes Remain High

That night our men slept in the open, close to the soil of our Cuba. Next morning we ate what rations we could gather from the villagers. We were set for another battle. But all was quiet for a time—except for the quarreling of vultures over the bodies of Castro's slain militiamen.

From Playa Larga, Oliva and his battalions had advanced more than 12 miles, fighting all the way. They had stopped 3,000 of Castro's militia, flanked by Russian tanks and covered by British-made Sea Fury planes. Our units had advanced almost that distance to the northeast. Realizing that our lines were too extended, San Roman ordered them pulled back.

Oliva began his withdrawal to join our forces north of Girón.

By noon of that second day, all officers and men realized it was then or never for victory. We had demoralized Castro's infantry with our deadly mortar and machine-gun fire. A few more days of pounding like that, and his forces would be surrendering in droves.

Colonel San Roman communicated with the American

ship: "Where is our support?" he asked. "We must have jet cover immediately."

The answer he got was nothing new—simply that we should advance and wait.

Ammunition Runs Low

All afternoon the enemy B-26s strafed and bombed us, while we looked in vain for the air support that could have knocked Castro's planes from the sky.

By nightfall, our forces had retreated from the Jagüey Grande area. Despite the terrific punishment from the air, we still held the terrain for six miles north of the bay, including the road junction at San Blas. We still stood guard over the airstrip on Girón Beach.

Keep advancing! Keep advancing—and wait!

But we were running out of ammunition. Every battalion reported it was running short of mortar shells, and even the small-arms bullets would soon be exhausted.

Meanwhile, from our advanced sentinels, we learned that Castro's forces were concentrating in huge numbers, with scores of tanks, hundreds of cannons and armored trucks, forming a ring of steel around the Bay of Pigs and getting ready to mount an attack.

Not a single plane from our bases had engaged the enemy during that second day of fighting.

The Troops Are Left Defenseless

At midmorning of the third day, we saw two of our B-26s winging in from over the water. Two Cuban planes zoomed out to meet them—one a Sea Fury, the other an American-made jet fighter—and within seconds our planes fell into the sea.

Soon afterward, three more of our planes flew over the beach and across the battle area. Two left quickly, but the third swooped down and began strafing the advancing Castro columns. Antiaircraft shells converged on that plane and it crashed. We found later that the pilot was Leo Francis Berle of Boston, an American instructor from the Nicaragua base. Early that morning he had learned that the invasion forces were to be abandoned to their fate. Apparently, in anger and frustration, he had determined to uphold his own honor, at least.

One of Oliva's radiomen kept repeating this message: "This is Cuba calling the free countries. We need help in Cuba—now!"

Like the coils of a great python, Castro's columns, with thousands of men supported by Russian tanks and bombing planes, were encircling our units and pressing them back toward the beach. We were outnumbered 40 to 1.

There can be no adequate description for the emotions that gripped us as we thought of what those planes on the U.S.S. *Boxer*, those guns on the two destroyers that had escorted us, and all our sunken mines and ammunition could do for us.

Manuel Artime Buesa and I were close by Colonel San Roman during the final hours of our defeat. We heard him make his last anguished plea for help.

"Where is our support?" he asked.

From far away in the ocean came the reply:

"We cannot give you any further support. You are on your own."

Quickly, in the anger of a leader forsaken, San Roman replied:

"And you, sir, are a s— of a b——"

As the coils of Castro's python strangled us, one of our men shouted: "Headquarters says it's every man for himself."

Penabaz and Others Escape

I had resigned myself to being captured when I ran into Rene Salvia, a boyhood friend from my home town. "Follow me!" he shouted. We ran to the beach. Several lifeboats were filling with men and pushing out to sea. Howitzer shells were falling all around us. We spied a rubber raft floating near the shore—one used by frogmen to mark the route for our landing barges. It had an outboard motor and three oars. Rene and I piled into it, followed by Pepin Casals, Gardo Orlando and Perez Jemenez. The motor refused to start, so we rowed out to sea.

For four days we paddled and drifted. About 5 o'clock on the fifth afternoon a freighter, the *Luisse*, bound for Corpus Christi, Tex., plucked us from the sea. Eventually I returned to Miami.

Penabaz Learns the Truth

Since then, I have learned much from my friends in the Revolutionary Council about the invasion at the Bay of Pigs. I have learned that no preparations were made for our cooperation with the underground in Cuba. No campaign of civilian uprising and sabotage had been planned.

Both the U.S. military chiefs and the CIA blandly assumed that there was enough opposition to Fidel Castro inside Cuba to overthrow his regime, once the movement had been sparked by our invasion.

Our exile leaders reflect with great sorrow upon the fact that the U.S. decision to cancel the promised help to our invading forces included also a refusal to rescue our men and prevent their capture. Not even those in lifeboats or struggling in the water could be rescued. American naval personnel at Guantánamo heard our pleas for help, but, on orders from Washington, they could not move a vessel to assist.

It is known that Castro salvaged every item that went down with the *Houston* and the *Rio Escondido*—including our new secret communications system which, doubtless, now has been duplicated by every Communist military command in the world.

Fidel Castro convicted 1,179 of the captives of treason. Now his demands for ransom have been met.

From my comrades of the invasion I have had my belief confirmed that no payment of ransom was necessary. The cowardly dictator had his plane all warmed up and waiting during the recent missile crisis, ready to flee the country at the first military move by the United States.

For me and for my comrades, the question still remains unanswered:

Why were we denied the help that would have uprooted the seedbed of Communist power in the Western Hemisphere?

2

Kennedy's Indecisiveness Was Behind the Bay of Pigs Disaster

Jack Hawkins

Thirty-five years after the 1961 Bay of Pigs invasion, many documents that had been classified as private in the interest of national security were declassified by the U.S. government. Jack Hawkins, chief of the paramilitary staff of the Cuba Project, had taken an oath of silence on all of his activities involving the invasion. Following declassification, he finally had the opportunity to speak out about what he thought were the real reasons behind the Bay of Pigs failure. As second in command of the troops, Hawkins was responsible for training the men and developing strategies for the invasion; therefore, he had intimate knowledge of the decision-making process before, during, and after the invasion. In the following essay Hawkins explains the many errors made regarding the invasion. He describes the poor locations of the training camps, a lack of arms and ammunition given to the troops, inadequate air support, and a last-minute change in the invasion site. Ultimately, Hawkins argues that the Bay of Pigs failure was the result of President John F. Kennedy's unwillingness to publicly demonstrate U.S. support of the invasion, which led to Kennedy's inability to employ the best warfare strategies. In Hawkins's opinion, the project was doomed to failure before the troops ever landed at the Bay of Pigs.

Jack Hawkins, "Classified Disaster: The Bay of Pigs Operation Was Doomed by Presidential Indecisiveness and Lack of Commitment," *National Review*, December 31, 1996. Copyright © 1996 by National Review, Inc., 215 Lexington Avenue. New York, NY 10016. Reproduced by permission.

Thirty-five years ago [in 1961], 1,500 exiled Cuban patriots landed on the south coast of their country, at the Bay of Pigs, in a gallant effort to free Cuba from Communist rule. They were abandoned on the beach without the supplies, protection, and support that had been promised by their sponsor, the Government of the United States. They had no chance of succeeding in their mission, and nearly all of them were captured or killed.

Hawkins Explains His Role

For 35 years, bound by my oath not to reveal classified information, I kept silent about the fatal errors in judgment that led to this disaster. Now this information is no longer classified, and I believe the facts should be reported.

My involvement with the Cuba Project began during the [Dwight] Eisenhower Administration. In late August of 1960, the Commandant of the Marine Corps, General David Shoup, told me that the CIA had requested the services of a Marine officer to assist in the landing of a small force of Cuban exiles. I had the required experience in amphibious operations, and also in guerrilla warfare (Philippines, 1943), and so he was assigning me to the job. I reported to the CIA on September 1.

Conditions there were extremely crowded and became health-threatening as additional recruits arrived.

At the CIA, I was assigned duty as Chief of the Paramilitary Staff of the Cuba Project, responsible directly to the Chief of the Cuba Project, Mr. Jacob Esterline.

The Cuba Project

I soon learned that the Cuba Project had been initiated by President Eisenhower in January 1960, when it had become clear that Castro was a Communist bent not only on establishing a Communist state in Cuba but also on subverting other Latin American countries. President Eisenhower decided that Castro should be overthrown and directed the CIA to prepare plans to that end.

The concept of the operation, developed by the CIA before my arrival, involved training paramilitary teams of

Cuban exiles to be introduced secretly back into their country for purposes of intelligence, sabotage, propaganda, and political and guerrilla activity. Each team would have a radio capable of communicating with the United States. It was planned also to form a small infantry force of 200 to 300 men that could be sent in to augment guerrilla activity fostered by the teams.

Unsafe Training Camp Locations

The project was flawed from the outset owing to diplomatic/political considerations. The safest and most efficient venues for both training camps and bases of operations would have been in the United States or Puerto Rico. However, the CIA was anxious not to have the operation appear to be run by the United States, and so training camps and airfields were established in Guatemala and Nicaragua, at extremely unsuitable locations. The training camp in Guatemala was located on the side of a remote volcano with very little level ground. Conditions there were extremely crowded and became health-threatening as additional recruits arrived. And from the airfield in Nicaragua chosen for tactical air operations, Cuba was just barely within range of the B-26 bombers procured by the CIA for the exile air force.

If the Cuban forces had been trained here, they could have been ready for action months earlier than they were, an important consideration. While the preparations continued, the Soviet Union was pouring great quantities of arms and other matériel into Cuba, enabling Castro to organize and equip large militia forces and consolidate his security system for control of the Cuban people. In view of these rapidly growing capabilities, the Deputy Director for Plans at the CIA, Mr. Richard Bissell, decided that the planned infantry force of 200 to 300 would not be large enough; more like 1,500 men would be needed to establish a serious presence in Cuba. I expressed reservations about a force this large in view of the increased difficulties in recruiting, training, and providing support. However, President Eisenhower directed that preparations be made for a larger force.

Lack of Arms and Ammunition

In late 1960 and early 1961, teams of paramilitary agents were landed in many places on the Cuban coast. Most of the teams established radio communication with the CIA, but some were captured immediately and never heard from again. The surviving teams reported that there were large numbers of men in all provinces of Cuba who were willing to fight against Castro if they were armed. The CIA tried to supply arms and ammunition to some of the teams by nocturnal parachute drops, but without success. The Cuban pilots were not experienced enough for these difficult missions, and our request for permission to use American contract pilots was denied, again so that the U.S. would not appear to be too deeply involved. The only sizable delivery of arms through the efforts of the agent teams was made by sea to a 400-man guerrilla unit operating in the Escambray mountains of central Cuba. About 1,000 guerrillas operated in this area in separate groups for many months.

Kennedy's First Mistake

Soon after President Kennedy's inauguration, Mr. Bissell briefed him about the Cuba Project. The new President was interested and scheduled a series of meetings at the White House involving the Secretary of State, Mr. Dean Rusk; the Secretary of Defense, Mr. Robert McNamara; the Chairman of the Joint Chiefs of Staff, Gen. Lymah Lemnitzer; and Mr. Bissell. Each of these officials brought assistants to these meetings, and I usually accompanied Mr. Bissell.

President Kennedy emphasized that operations would have to be conducted in such a way that U.S. involvement could be "plausibly deniable."

President Kennedy emphasized that operations would have to be conducted in such a way that U.S. involvement could be "plausibly deniable." This was the fundamental mistake underlying the other fatal errors that led to the failure of the operation. It should have been apparent to all concerned that the recruiting of large numbers of Cubans in Miami, followed by the landing of a well-armed Cuban exile force in Cuba with air support, would be attributed to the United States. If that was held to be unacceptable, the operation should have been canceled; if it was not canceled, it should have received the support required for success. As it was, the Administration neither escaped blame nor succeeded in liberating Cuba.

Inadequate Air Support

The crucial point at issue was air support. Throughout my participation in the Cuba Project, I frequently emphasized, both orally and in formal correspondence, the absolute necessity for complete destruction of the opposing air force at the outset of the operation. In January 1961, in a memorandum to higher CIA authority, I recommended that the landing operation be canceled if sufficient air operations were not to be allowed. In another memorandum in early 1961, I stated flatly that if Castro's aircraft were not all destroyed before the troop transports arrived at the landing beaches, a military disaster would occur. An unarmed freighter cannot approach a hostile shore, drop anchor, and unload troops, supplies, and equipment while under fighter and bomber attack. Mr. Rusk did not seem to grasp this point. At the White House meetings, it became clear that he was unalterably opposed to any air operations whatsoever. To my surprise and chagrin, neither Mr. McNamara nor Gen. Lemnitzer spoke up in these meetings in defense of the necessity of eliminating Castro's air force completely by preliminary air strikes. And so, when the recommendations of the State Department conflicted with those of the CIA, the President usually adopted Mr. Rusk's position.

Absolute control of the air was essential not only for the landing but also for further operations in Cuba. Our Cuban Brigade was small and could not be expected to undertake operations beyond its initial lodgement unless the strength of the opposing militia was seriously reduced by combat losses—or by defection to our side. Many of the militia were of dubious loyalty to Castro and might well have turned against him had this operation been properly launched.

Absolute control of the air was essential not only for the landing but also for further operations in Cuba.

As the spring of 1961 approached, the Brigade, now up to planned strength, and its supporting tactical air force of 16 B-26s were nearing readiness for combat. Commercial freighters were chartered for the operation, four for the assault phase and three for follow-on delivery of supplies.

Meanwhile, the time element was becoming critical. The Soviet Union continued delivering arms and equipment to Cuba and was training jet pilots for Castro in Eastern Europe. Soon Castro would have a modern jet air force, and a paramilitary effort to overthrow him would have no chance of success.

Kennedy Vetoes the Landing Site

After long study, the Paramilitary Staff had concluded that by far the best place, and probably the only place, where a successful landing (i.e., one likely to lead to the overthrow of Castro) could be made was at Trinidad near the middle of the southern coast of Cuba. Good landing beaches were available very near the Escambray mountains, where, as noted above, anti-Castro guerrillas were already operating. The Brigade could quickly establish itself in these mountains and incorporate the guerrillas already there.

Trinidad itself had a population of about 18,000, offering the possibility of recruiting additional volunteers. Our agent teams had informed us that most of the people in the area were opposed to Castro.

The Paramilitary Staff prepared a complete plan for the Trinidad operation, which was presented to the President and his advisors. Mr. Rusk strongly opposed the plan, saying that it was too much like an invasion and too easily attributable to the United States. He thought the Soviet Union might be provoked to the extent of taking action against the United States in Berlin or elsewhere in the world.

Once again, the President agreed with Mr. Rusk. He rejected the Trinidad plan and directed that a plan be developed that would be less noisy and less like an invasion. He also adopted the restriction advanced by Mr. Rusk that an airfield capable of supporting B-26 operations would have to be captured on the first day so that all air operations could be attributed to that field.

This was the first fatal error made by President Kennedy: rejecting a plan that offered a good chance of success and placing "plausible deniability" ahead of military viability.

The Bay of Pigs Becomes the New Landing Site

Pursuant to Mr. Bissell's oral instructions to me, the Paramilitary Staff studied the entire coast of Cuba in an effort to find a landing area that would satisfy the President's requirements. We found that the only place on the Cuban coast which did so and could be held even for a minimal time was at the Bahia de Cochinos (Bay of Pigs).

I reported this orally to Mr. Bissell and briefly described the area. Behind the beach lay a long narrow strip of flat, scrub-covered land from three to six miles in depth and forty miles wide. This land was cut off from the interior by a great swamp, impassable except for three narrow causeways approaching the beach from the north and a coastal road from the east, all of which could probably be blocked for a time by the Brigade (and on the other side of the swamp by Castro's militia).

It had become obvious that the military requirements for a successful operation and the President's insistence on plausible deniability were in irreconcilable conflict.

I pointed out to Mr. Bissell that the Brigade could hold on there for only a limited time and would have no hope of breaking out through the swamp and reaching guerrilla country in the Escambray mountains eighty miles away. However, since the Bay of Pigs was the only place that met the President's requirements, Mr. Bissell decided on the spot that we would have to go ahead on that basis. This was another fatal error, as Mr. Bissell later acknowledged, lamenting that he had never informed the President that landing at the Bay of Pigs ruled out the possibility of guerrilla warfare in the Escambray mountains.

Our plan for the Bay of Pigs landing provided for an attack on three Cuban military airfields by 16 B-26 bombers on April 15, the landing itself during darkness in the early morning of April 17, and a second 16-bomber attack against the military airfields at first light on April 17. The President approved the plan and directed that all preparations continue. However, he also stated that he would not finally decide whether to execute the operation until 24 hours before it was scheduled to begin.

Bissell Refuses to Abandon the Invasion

Not long after this, the Chief of the Cuba Project, Mr. Esterline, and I had a serious talk about the outlook for the

Bay of Pigs operation and found ourselves in complete agreement that it was certain to fail. We went to Mr. Bissell at his home on a Sunday to attempt to dissuade him from continuing with the operation. We even went so far as to say that we did not want to be parties to the disaster we believed lay ahead.

Mr. Bissell tried to reassure us and implored us not to let him down. He said he thought he could persuade the President to permit an increase in our air capability to ensure destruction of Castro's air force. But he gave no assurance about other weaknesses of the plan.

With their supply ships either sunk or chased away, the troops eventually ran out of ammunition and had to surrender.

I thought that after hearing unequivocal predictions of complete disaster from his two principal staff officers who were most familiar with the military aspects of the plan, Mr. Bissell would re-examine the whole operation. It had become obvious that the military requirements for a successful operation and the President's insistence on plausible deniability were in irreconcilable conflict. However, Mr. Bissell could not bring himself to give up on the plan. This was another fatal error.

The Attack on Castro's Air Force Fails

On April 14, devastating instructions came from the White House. The President informed Mr. Bissell that he wanted the number of participating aircraft reduced to the minimum. Mr. Bissell, without consulting Mr. Esterline or me, volunteered to cut the number by half, from 16 to 8—although 16 was considered the minimal number for destroying 18 opposing aircraft scattered on three different fields. The President accepted Mr. Bissell's offer. Military failure was now virtually assured.

The attack was carried out the next morning with only eight B-26s, and our fears were confirmed when post-strike photography revealed that half of Castro's military aircraft, including five fighters, had escaped destruction. These posed a deadly threat to the landing and to our B-26s as well.

News of the attack spread rapidly. At the United Nations, Ambassador Adlai Stevenson, a leading figure in the Democratic Party, who had not been informed about the operation, denied U.S. involvement. When he learned the truth, he was outraged and protested to the President that this affair was extremely embarrassing both to the President and to him. He was reinforced in that position by Mr. Rusk.

Kennedy Cancels the Second Strike

This led the President to make another decision, which made disaster absolutely certain. I was in the CIA operations room at about 10 P.M. on April 16, three hours before the troops were to commence landing, when Mr. Esterline hurried in with an ashen face and told me that the President had canceled the second attack on Castro's air force, the one scheduled for first light the next morning. Appalled, I rushed to the telephone and called Mr. Bissell, who was at the State Department, and urged him in the strongest terms to call the President and explain that the invasion force faced certain destruction unless the order was reversed. I predicted that our troop transports would be under air attack and some or all would be sunk.

After my plea, Mr. Bissell and General C.P. Cabell, the Deputy Director of the CIA, spoke to Mr. Rusk. He telephoned the President, who had left Washington, and told him that the CIA wanted to reinstate the air strike but that he believed the decision should not be changed. McGeorge Bundy, the National Security Advisor, seconded Mr. Rusk's advice. The cancellation remained in effect.

This final incredible mistake doomed Brigade 2506 [the CIA-trained militia]. The President himself had initially approved the original operation plan, which provided for forty B-26 sorties in preliminary air strikes. After his last-minute cuts, only eight sorties were flown, a reduction of 80 per cent.

Brigade 2506 Suffers Heavy Losses

While Washington floundered, the troops of Brigade 2506 landed successfully in darkness. But when morning came, Castro's fighters and bombers attacked, and they continued to attack all day. Unloading supplies from the ships was impossible. Two ships were sunk, and the remaining two had to flee at top speed.

The Brigade fought hard and well for three days and was not overrun or driven from its position. With their supply ships either sunk or chased away, the troops eventually ran out of ammunition and had to surrender.

During three days of combat, from 3,000 to 4,000 casualties were inflicted upon Castro's hard-core militia, mostly by B-26 attacks on troop convoys. The hard-core militia, the only troops trusted by Castro, were limited in number and could not long have endured casualties of such magnitude.

Before the surrender, Admiral Arleigh "31-knot" Burke, the Chief of Naval Operations, requested permission from the President to have carrier aircraft eliminate the rest of Castro's air force and fly cover and support for the Brigade, and to use Navy landing craft to evacuate the troops from the beach. The President refused.

It was noteworthy that when the Brigade landed, the defending militia unit fought little and surrendered quickly. About 150 men were captured, and nearly all volunteered to join the Brigade and fight against Castro. Civilians in the landing area also volunteered to help the Brigade.

These facts confirmed that our concept of the operation had merit, and that, if the landing had been made at Trinidad as recommended, and with adequate air support, the objective of overthrowing the Communist government might well have been accomplished.

But, as things turned out, Brigade 2506 was left stranded on the beach, shamefully misled and betrayed by the Government of the United States. The last message from José "Pepe" San Román, the Brigade Commander, was, "How can you people do this to us?"

The Aftermath of the Invasion

Less than four months into the Kennedy Administration, the Bay of Pigs fiasco caused the U.S. Government to be perceived as weak, irresolute, and inept. Undoubtedly, [Soviet] Chairman [Nikita] Khrushchev was reassured that he had little to fear from the United States as he pressed on with his plans to turn Cuba into a Soviet armed camp.

If those plans had been aborted at the outset, there would have been no missile crisis bringing us to the brink of nuclear war, and Cuba would be a free and prosperous country today.

3

Conflicting Viewpoints in the Kennedy Administration Led to the Bay of Pigs Defeat

U.S. News & World Report

In this selection a *U.S. News & World Report* reporter investigates the reasons for the failure at the Bay of Pigs, revealing that disputes within John F. Kennedy's administration resulted in delays in carrying through with the plan. The "actionists" advocated direct action in Cuba, while the "how-not-to-do-it crowd" advised more conservative actions. As these battling factions caused more delays, Communist military aid poured into Cuba and strengthened the Cuban army, helping to ensure the defeat of the CIA-trained anti-Castro militia at the Bay of Pigs. In this article, published in May 1961, less than a month after the invasion, the author argues that the United States must take the next step and remove Cuban dictator Fidel Castro from office. Part of that next step involves creating an organization in addition to the CIA to carry out covert operations. Ultimately, the United States must persist in accomplishing its anti-Castro goals or be willing to accept that Cuba has been taken over by Communists.

The story of the effort to unseat Fidel Castro goes back to March, 1960. That was when the important decision was made by the [Dwight] Eisenhower Administration

"Where U.S. Went Wrong on Cuba," *U.S. News & World Report*, May 8, 1961, pp. 54–56.

that Castro was a hopeless captive of Communism—and had to go.

This story is just now coming to light. It comes from persons on the inside, in a position to know all the factors that went into that decision.

Nixon's Role in the Invasion

Richard Nixon, former Vice President, played a prominent role in the development of the plan under the Eisenhower Administration. He was intimately acquainted with the plans of the Eisenhower Administration and has been kept informed of what has been done since the Kennedy Administration took over the Cuban problem. Mr. Nixon was briefed by President John F. Kennedy on April 20.

Now, from what Mr. Nixon has been telling his friends and from other informed sources, it is possible to gain a new insight into what actually happened in Cuba—and why.

Communist arms, tanks, and jet planes were pouring into Cuba.

This inside story shows that the anti-Castro invasion of Cuba which was attempted on April 17 had been building up for more than a year.

As early as the spring of 1959—only a few months after Castro seized power from Dictator [Fulgencio] Batista in Cuba—some high officials in the Eisenhower Administration were beginning to warn about the communistic trend of the Cuban dictator's course.

Understanding Castro

In April, 1959, Castro came to Washington to address the American Society of Newspaper Editors. During that visit, the then Vice President, Mr. Nixon, talked with Castro for three hours. After that talk Mr. Nixon wrote a memorandum evaluating Castro as a captive of Communism. The memorandum was distributed among top people in the Eisenhower Administration.

At that time, however, there was great division within the State Department as to Castro's real nature, and Mr. Nixon's view was in the minority. The prevailing view in the State Department was that Castro could be saved.

Finally, in March, 1960, Mr. Nixon's view prevailed. The State Department, at the top level, came around to the conclusion that Castro was hopelessly a captive of the Communists, and that something had to be done about him.

Training the Guerrilla Forces

It was then that the decision was made to start training a guerrilla force of Cubans to overthrow the dictator.

The Central Intelligence Agency drew up the plans and directed the training operations.

Training of the Cuban guerrilla force continued and grew through the summer of 1960 and the presidential-election campaign of that autumn.

In the election campaign, presidential candidate John Kennedy complained that the Eisenhower Administration was not doing enough about Castro. He advocated open aid to the rebels.

Mr. Kennedy was then briefed personally by Allen Dulles, head of the CIA, about what the Administration was doing and about the thinking behind that action.

Kennedy's and Nixon's Opposing Views

During the presidential campaign, Mr. Nixon's position was different from that of Mr. Kennedy. The Republican nominee [Nixon] felt that direct and open aid to anti-Castro Cubans would be held in violation of this country's treaty obligations. He favored covert, or undercover, aid.

When Mr. Kennedy became President, on January 20, one of his first acts was to retain as head of CIA the man who was in over-all direction of the anti-Castro operation—Allen Dulles. Training of Cuban guerillas continued.

The Cuban Debate

President Kennedy soon found, however, that there existed within his own Administration the same dispute that had delayed action by the Eisenhower Administration against Castro.

On one side were the "actionists" who advocated doing something positive to get rid of Castro. On this side were the CIA and high military chiefs.

On the other side were those who came to be known as the "how-not-to-do-it crowd," who kept warning about what should not be done. In this group were high officials in the State Department and some key aides in the White House. . . .

Arguments against going into Cuba included these: Action involving the United States would provoke resentment in Latin America, lose this country friends in many parts of the world. It might provoke Soviet Russia to intervene—perhaps even touch off World War III. Or Russia might retaliate by engineering a coup in Laos or Iran. And—the action against Castro might fail.

The dispute within the Kennedy Administration resulted in delay. Meanwhile Communist arms, tanks, and jet planes were pouring into Cuba. Castro's military strength grew.

Eventually, despite the cautionings of his "how not to do it" advisers, President Kennedy decided to go ahead with some of the plans that had been taking shape ever since March of 1960.

Kennedy's Restrictions

Mr. Kennedy, however, tied some strings to the operation. One of these strings was that no American troops or planes were to become involved. Another restriction consisted of the President's declaration of the world that the U.S. would not intervene militarily in Cuba.

Without military support from the U.S., and without a mass uprising by the Cuban people, the invasion failed.

What went wrong?

The former Vice President, in talking to friends, has made it plain that he is not trying to criticize President Kennedy or to second guess him. Mr. Nixon has expressed praise for the courage of the President in doing what he did in the face of a great deal of opposition among his top advisers.

The CIA Needs an Overhaul

What is regarded as important now are the next moves.

Mr. Nixon is known to feel that the United States cannot afford to sit back, as some advisers have been suggesting, and wait for the "food for peace" program to solve the Communist problem in Latin America—or the problem of Laos, either.

The United States, he feels, must be prepared to act.

It can also be said that Mr. Nixon is convinced that some

kind of paramilitary operations are needed to cope with the kind of indirect aggression that the Communists are waging. By "paramilitary" is meant operations that are somewhat military in nature but do not involve direct use of U.S. armed forces. Such was the type of operation in Cuba.

One thing is known to be viewed by Mr. Nixon as the worst possible mistake that the U.S. could make. That is to wash its hands of paramilitary operations as a result of the fiasco in Cuba.

A complete overhaul of the CIA is seen as vital.

Instead, the Nixon idea is that the quality of this country's paramilitary operations should be improved—so that they will not fail. This country's program for dealing with indirect aggression is called "woefully inadequate."

To develop an effective program of paramilitary operations, it is Mr. Nixon's view that some new kind of organization is needed. The Central Intelligence Agency is regarded, in its present form, as not equipped for the job. A complete overhaul of the CIA is seen as vital.

The suggestion is to divide the present functions of the CIA—let it continue to gather intelligence information, but have a different agency carry out undercover operations.

The Government Must Take the Next Step

Looking at operations such as that in Cuba, Mr. Nixon is described as stressing one necessity: willingness on the part of the U.S. President to take the "second step."

It is recalled that, in 1958, when President Eisenhower decided to send marines into Lebanon to forestall a Communist coup, Mr. Eisenhower asked the then Secretary of State, John Foster Dulles: "Are you ready to take the second step?" Mr. Dulles nodded.

That "second step" is described as doing whatever is necessary to win, in case unexpectedly strong opposition is met. The idea is expressed that, once American prestige is committed to an undertaking such as that in Cuba, a President has to be prepared to follow through—the operation must not be allowed to fail.

This thinking is applied to Laos, as well as to Cuba.

What about "collective action" by the Organization of

American States against Castro?

From his experience with Latin America, Mr. Nixon is pictured as convinced that "multilateral" action can never be effective against Castro—because Latin-American leaders fear him, fear the mobs that can be stirred up against themselves, and are afraid to take any initiative.

The Nixon view is that the U.S. will have to take the initiative—act as trustee for the American nations and stabilize the situation by unilateral action, until other signatories to the Latin-American pacts join in support.

It is pointed out that the U.N. charter provides for unilateral action when a nation's security is challenged.

Cuba and the Second Step

As to the type of "second step" to be taken against Castro, Mr. Nixon is reported as feeling that President Kennedy is in a good position to move either way in supporting anti-Castro forces: either through covert paramilitary operations or by more direct action, if developments make that necessary.

As Communist arms continue to pour into Cuba and as the likelihood grows of threatening action by Cuba against her neighbors, the possibility is seen that the U.S. may be placed in a position where it will clearly be compelled to act in defense of its own security.

On one thing, Mr. Nixon is reported as being firmly convinced: The U.S. cannot afford any more Cuba failures. If Castro is allowed many more months of build-up, Cuba can be written off as a loss to Communism.

4

The CIA Could Not Adequately Handle the Bay of Pigs Operation

Lyman Kirkpatrick

Following a six-month internal investigation, CIA inspector general Lyman Kirkpatrick issued his report concerning the Bay of Pigs invasion. His report angered many senior officials, and the CIA director, John McCone, ordered all but one copy of it destroyed. The report remained stored in the CIA director's safe from October 1961 until 1998, when the National Security Archive at George Washington University obtained it for its collection. In the section included here, Kirkpatrick lays out nine points that describe the failure of the CIA to successfully carry out the invasion. He argues that the CIA was underprepared for a task of this nature and lacked the intelligence information and understanding of Fidel Castro's capabilities that were crucial to successfully carrying out the plan. His final recommendations to the CIA include the need for better organization and management, the development of a task force, and the creation of clearly defined policies and plans, all modeled after the lessons learned from the Bay of Pigs invasion.

Certain basic *conclusions* have been drawn from this survey of the Cuban operation:

1. The Central Intelligence Agency, after starting to build up the resistance and guerrilla forces inside Cuba, drastically converted the project into what

Lyman Kirkpatrick, "Inspector General's Survey of the Cuban Operation, October 1961."

rapidly became an overt military operation. The Agency failed to recognize that when the project advanced beyond the stage of plausible denial it was going beyond the area of Agency responsibility as well as Agency capability.

2. The Agency became so wrapped up in the military operation that it failed to appraise the chances of success realistically. Furthermore, it failed to keep the national policy-makers adequately and realistically informed of the conditions considered essential for success, and it did not press sufficiently for prompt policy decisions in a fast moving situation.

3. As the project grew, the Agency reduced the exiled leaders to the status of puppets, thereby losing the advantages of their active participation.

4. The Agency failed to build up and supply a resistance organization under rather favorable conditions. Air and boat operations showed up poorly.

5. The Agency failed to collect adequate information on the strengths of the Castro regime and the extent of the opposition to it; and it failed to evaluate the available information correctly.

6. The project was badly organized. Command lines and management controls were ineffective and unclear. . . .

7. The project was not staffed throughout with top-quality people, and a number of people were not used to the best advantage.

8. The Agency entered the project without adequate assets in the way of boats, bases, training facilities, agent nets, Spanish-speakers, and similar essential ingredients of a successful operation. Had these been already in being, much time and effort would have been saved.

9. Agency policies and operational plans were never clearly delineated, with the exception of the plan for the brigade landing; but even this provided no disaster plan, no unconventional warfare annex, and only extremely vague plans for action following a successful landing. In general, Agency plans and policies did not precede the various operations in the project but were drawn up in response to operational needs as they arose. Consequently, the scope of the operation itself and of the support required was constantly shifting.

Positive Aspects

There were some good things in this project. Much of the support provided was outstanding (for example, logistics and communications). A number of individuals did superior jobs. Many people at all grade levels gave their time and effort without stint, working almost unlimited hours over long periods, under difficult and frustrating conditions, without regard to personal considerations. But this was not enough.

Final Recommendations

It is assumed that the Agency, because of its experience in this Cuban operation, will never again engage in an operation that is essentially an overt military effort. But before it takes on another major covert political operation it will have to improve its organization and management drastically. It must find a way to set up an actual task force, if necessary, and be able to staff it with the best people. It must govern its operation with clearly defined policies and carefully drawn plans, engaging in full coordination with the Departments of State and Defense as appropriate.

5

Kennedy Was Responsible for the Bay of Pigs Failure

Jack Skelly

Longtime United Press International reporter Jack Skelly chronicled the early years of Cuban leader Fidel Castro's rise to power. In this essay he explores the causes of the Bay of Pigs failure by interviewing a few survivors of Brigade 2506, the CIA-trained militia that fought against Castro. Although the United States supported their anti-Castro sentiments and helped them escape Castro's control, the survivors hold President John F. Kennedy directly responsible for the invasion's failure. They argue that Kennedy did not follow through with his promises to support the brigade. At the last minute, the antirevolutionaries discovered that they were lacking in ammunition and in air support. Skelly also notes that many U.S. citizens believe that no Americans were involved or injured in the invasion, but four American pilots were killed. In addition, although the press and other sources often blame the CIA for bungling the operation, Skelly contends that it was President Kennedy's personal decisions that led to the defeat.

The 1961 effort to overthrow Cuban dictator Fidel Castro failed miserably, and fingers were pointed at the CIA. But was it the president who deceived the American people?

The ignominious failure of John F. Kennedy's invasion of Cuba at the Bay of Pigs on April 17, 1961, has faded in

Jack Skelly, "Ducking the Blame at the Bay of Pigs," *Insight on the News*, vol. 15, April 26, 1999, p. 45. Copyright © 1999 by News World Communications, Inc. All rights reserved. Reproduced by permission.

national memory. The JFK acolytes have blamed the CIA, the Joint Chiefs of Staff, the superiority of the Castro forces or the "Mickey Mouse" anti-Castro brigades that allegedly bungled the effort. But to the survivors of that expedition, there is little doubt about the blame.

Every year on April 17, at one minute past midnight, the honor guard of the Bay of Pigs Brigade begins a vigil before their "monument of heroes" at 13th Avenue and Calle Ocho (Eighth Street) in the heart of Little Havana in Miami. President of the Brigade Juan Perez Franco reads the names of each of the 100-some Cuban freedom fighters who died in combat on land, at sea and in the air. As each name is called, the veterans, family and friends respond, "Presente!" Present!

"President Kennedy is responsible for the humiliating defeat. There is no room for argument there."

According to the 70-year-old Perez Franco, 1,400 freedom fighters of the Cuban Expeditionary Forces, or CEF, went ashore that morning. Including 18 pilots, maintenance crews and others, a total of 2,700 Cubans were involved in the entire operation: Of these, 108 were killed in action, and nine more were asphyxiated in a prisoner trailer taking them to Havana jails. After the brigadistas were released in exchange for $62 million worth of medicines—which Castro reshipped in December 1962 to Communist countries to satisfy debts—700 of the CEF freedom fighters joined the U.S. armed forces. Today they have the right to Veterans Administration hospital care but receive no pensions. About 400 of these veterans since have died.

Invasion Survivors Blame Kennedy

But ask any of the Bay of Pigs survivors who was responsible for the debacle, and each gives the same answer. Perez Franco, a paratrooper who commanded the 150 men of the 1st Paratrooper Battalion, says: "We are eternally grateful to this country for the way they treated Cubans fleeing Castro's communism. However, President Kennedy is responsible for the humiliating defeat. There is no room for argument there."

On the fourth day of the invasion, when it was obvious that the operation had failed, Kennedy accepted blame for the disaster in an address to the American Association of Newspaper Editors. He then sent his spin doctors to lunch at expensive Washington restaurants with influential columnists, radio commentators and TV reporters to make sure the word got out that those to blame were a bumbling CIA, an incompetent Joint Chiefs of Staff—and the poorly trained and lightly armed Cubans. JFK was quoted to the favored journalists, off the record, of course, as saying, "How could I have been so stupid" to trust such a gang?

But despite this spin, still widely accepted as true, the historical facts are otherwise. And, they at once are attainable and readily confirmed by documents since declassified.

The Invasion Plan

The invasion plan on which Kennedy signed off called for the following:

On the morning of April 15 (D Minus 2, two days before the invasion) 18 B-26 planes flown in groups of six by experienced Cuban pilots would bomb Castro's air force on the ground at three locations: Havana, San Antonio de los Banos and Santiago, Cuba's second-largest city. The planes also would bomb and strafe bridges and communication towers on their way back to their base in Nicaragua. After refueling, the same group that afternoon was supposed to finish off what was left of Castro's tiny air force. To be absolutely certain that none of Castro's planes survived to strike the vulnerable invading forces and supply ships, the plan called for hitting the same airfields at 6 o'clock on the morning of the invasion.

"The air above the beaches will be yours," the CIA, U.S. Army and Marine officers training the Cubans repeatedly told the volunteers. In fact, this was the one condition that the Joint Chiefs demanded before they signed off on the invasion. Nonetheless the Kennedy apologists, led by "the best and the brightest" of the New Frontiersmen [Kennedy administration officials], including Arthur Schlesinger Jr., Theodore Sorensen, McGeorge Bundy, Robert McNamara and Richard Goodwin, spread the canard that the president never promised the Cubans "U.S. air cover." Right enough, as the battle plan called for strikes not by the United States but by the exile air group. The mythmakers also told carefully selected members of a flattered press that JFK never promised that the Marines would be right behind the Cuban invaders. Indeed not, for that wasn't part of the battle plan either. Neither was it part of the plan for the exile invaders to run out of ammunition because Castro's tiny air force survived to sink two ships carrying ammunition, trucks, tanks, communication equipment and 15,000 rifles and ammo intended to arm the Cuban people.

When the freedom fighters ran out of ammunition on the third day, they had to surrender or die.

Kennedy had not promised "U.S. air cover," but he had guaranteed the bombing of Castro's air force by Cuban pilots. That was at once crucial and essential. But only hours before the first bombings, JFK ordered the number of planes in the strike force reduced by half—only three per airfield.

"With six planes per airfield, we would have destroyed all of Castro's planes on the first day, April 15," experienced pilot Rene Garcia tells *Insight* [journal]. "Instead, two of our planes were shot down, killing the pilots and crew, and we only got 60 percent of Castro's planes on the three airfields. How in the hell did they expect us to bomb and strafe with only three planes per airfield?"

Garcia, who later flew for the CIA in Africa, says that it got worse. When they returned to their base after a two-hour-and-20-minute flight each way—allowing only 20 minutes over the target—they got new orders: "All bombings for today and tomorrow have been canceled by President Kennedy."

And that was not the end of the story, says Garcia. At 9 P.M. on Sunday, April 16, or D Minus 1, Kennedy called off the remaining bombings and strafings of Castro's air force scheduled for 6 o'clock the next morning.

The Invasion Fails

The invasion began at 1 A.M. with the first troops going ashore at the Bay of Pigs and six planes of Castro's air force surviving. Two T-33 jet trainers with rockets and 50-caliber machine guns sank the invasion ships and downed the slow B-26s over the Bay of Pigs. When the freedom fighters ran out of ammunition on the third day, they had to surrender or die.

The U.S. aircraft carrier *Essex*, with 60 planes aboard, was 10 miles off shore, along with nearly 18 other U.S. Navy ships. Adm. Arleigh Burke, then chief of naval operations, testified later that he was confident that if the invasion forces had complete control of "the air over the beaches" they would have defeated Castro's militia. Indeed, at least 350 of the militia joined the invaders during the three days of fighting. Thanks to manipulation of the secrecy acts, however, Kennedy's orders to pull out the linchpin of the strategic plan, the air strikes by the exiles, remained tightly sealed throughout the period in which the New Frontiersmen produced their self-serving histories and memoirs. But in April 1985 the JFK Library at Harvard University released the "annexes" of the closed inquiry conducted for Kennedy by Gen. Maxwell D. Taylor immediately after the defeat.

Documents Reveal Kennedy Is to Blame

The transcripts of the Bay of Pigs testimony had been published as *Ultrasensitive Report and Testimony, Operation Zapata* by University Publications of America in April 1981. But it is those "annexes" that carry the meat of the testimony by Kennedy-administration officials as well as by the surviving Cuban freedom fighters. Titled *Paramilitary Study: Ultrasensitive, Eyes Only*, the annexes contain more than 30 sections amounting to 150 pages.

Section 21 is the key document that reveals beyond doubt that, without consulting the CIA or the Joint Chiefs, Kennedy personally called off the last bombing scheduled for 6 A.M. on April 17. A four-page, single-spaced memorandum to Taylor dated May 9, 1961, from Gen. C.P. Cabell, CIA deputy director, details the events of the night of April 16 leading up to the Kennedy order canceling the essential early-morning bombings. Cabell writes that the Cuban-exile pilots already were in the cockpits of their planes preparing to take off when the order came from the White House.

Section 18 of the document completely contradicts the New Frontier myth that the exiles were a group of stumblebum oafs. A Marine colonel, sent by the president for a final look at the preparedness of the invasion team, reported as follows:

"My observations the last few days have increased my

confidence in the ability of this force to accomplish not only initial combat missions, but also the ultimate objective of Castro's overthrow. . . . The Brigade is well organized and is more heavily armed and better equipped in some respects than U.S. Infantry units. The men have received intensive training in the use of their weapons, including more firing experience than U.S. troops would normally receive. I was impressed with the serious attitude of the men as they arrived here and moved to their ships. Movements were quiet, disciplined and efficient, and the embarkation was accomplished with remarkable smoothness. . . . The Brigade officers do not expect help from U.S. Armed Forces. They ask only for contained delivery of supplies. This can be done covertly."

Kennedy Calls Off the Air Strike

Thirty-five years after writing this memo, Marine Col. Jack Hawkins broke silence in an article in the Dec. 31, 1996, edition of *National Review:*

"The crucial point at issue was air support. Throughout my participation in the Cuba project I frequently emphasized both orally and in formal correspondence the absolute necessity for complete destruction of the opposing air force at the outset of the operation. In another memorandum in early 1961 I stated flatly that if Castro's air force were not all destroyed before the troop transports arrived at the landing beaches, a military disaster would occur. . . . [Secretary of State Dean] Rusk did not seem to grasp the point . . . so when the recommendations from the State Department conflicted with those of the CIA, the President usually adopted Mr. Rusk's position. . . . President Kennedy's cancelling of the invasion bombing of the remains of Castro's air force doomed Brigade 2506. . . . The Brigade fought hard and well for three days and was not overrun or driven from its position. . . . The troops eventually ran out of ammunition and had to surrender. Before the surrender . . . [Admiral Arleigh] Burke requested permission from the President to have carrier aircraft eliminate the rest of Castro's air force and fly cover and support for the Brigade, and use naval landing craft to evacuate troops from the beach. The president refused."

Perez Franco tells *Insight* that Castro's artillery fired from the beaches on the nearby U.S. Navy ships. "Instead of returning fire," he says, "the ships kept moving backward." As a result, Hawkins wrote: "Brigade 2506 was left stranded on the beach, shamefully misled and betrayed by the government of the United States of America."

Why did Kennedy call off the final air strike? It appears from long-classified documents that U.S. Ambassador to the U.N. Adlai Stevenson, whom Kennedy had called a "national asset," was embarrassed at the United Nations by disclosure in the media of the first bombing on April 15. As the Cabell memorandum stated:

"The Secretary of State agreed that strikes could be made in the immediate beachhead area, but confirmed that the planned air strikes against Cuban air fields, a harbor, and a radio broadcasting station, could not be permitted and the decision to cancel would stand. He asked if I should like to speak to the President. Mr. Bissell and I were impressed with the extremely delicate situation with Ambassador Stevenson and the United Nations and the risk to the entire political position of the United States, and the firm position of the Secretary. We saw no point in my speaking personally to the President and so informed the Secretary."

Kennedy Deceived the American People

Another part of the Kennedy myth was that no Americans participated or were killed at the Bay of Pigs. Yet the truth had been known immediately that four American pilots were killed. The Kennedy spinners smeared these patriotic men by calling them "hired civilian pilots," as though they were mercenaries. In fact, they were officers of the Alabama National Guard. Albert C. Persons of the Alabama Guard told the complete story of how his men were shot down by Castro's T-33 trainers in his 1968 book *The Bay of Pigs*. According to Persons: ". . . it was not the CIA who changed the invasion plans at the last minute; it was not the CIA who cancelled the air attacks vital to the success of the invasion; it was not the CIA who insisted on a 'quiet' landing 'preferably at night' and who cut down the strength of the initial attacks against Castro's air bases. It was not the CIA who sent the Cuban freedom fighters ashore on Monday morning without air cover, and it was not the CIA who deceived the American people."

Chapter 3

The Bay of Pigs Legacy

1

The United States Must Continue the Fight Against Communist Oppression

John F. Kennedy

Just four days after the Bay of Pigs invasion in 1961, President John F. Kennedy gave the following speech to the American Society of Newspaper Editors. He begins his address by briefly reiterating that the situation in Cuba has worsened and the invading troops have been defeated. He denies U.S. involvement in these failed actions but insists that should a threat ever arise against the security of the United States, then the government will use whatever means necessary to protect the country. He acknowledges the failure of the invasion and then goes on to explain three major lessons that the United States has learned from the failure. First, he argues that communism is the biggest threat facing the United States and that it should not be underestimated. The democratic world must further investigate Cuba as a potential site of global Communist activity. This struggle against communism should be relentless. Finally, Kennedy issues a call to arms in the dissolution of Communist power in Cuba and around the world, predicting that it will be defeated in the near future thanks in part to the efforts in the Bay of Pigs invasion.

John F. Kennedy, address before the American Society of Newspaper Editors, April 20, 1961.

82

The President of a great democracy such as ours, and the editors of great newspapers such as yours, owe a common obligation to the people: an obligation to present the facts, to present them with candor, and to present them in perspective. It is with that obligation in mind that I have decided in the last 24 hours to discuss briefly at this time the recent events in Cuba.

On that unhappy island, as in so many other arenas of the contest for freedom, the news has grown worse instead of better. I have emphasized before that this was a struggle of Cuban patriots against a Cuban dictator. While we could not be expected to hide our sympathies, we made it repeatedly clear that the armed forces of this country would not intervene in any way.

Necessary American Intervention

Any unilateral American intervention, in the absence of an external attack upon ourselves or an ally, would have been contrary to our traditions and to our international obligations. But let the record show that our restraint is not inexhaustible. Should it ever appear that the inter-American doctrine of noninterference merely conceals or excuses a policy of nonaction—if the nations of this Hemisphere should fail to meet their commitments against outside Communist penetration—then I want it clearly understood that this Government will not hesitate in meeting its primary obligations which are to the security of our Nation.

Let the record show that our restraint is not inexhaustible.

Should that time ever come, we do not intend to be lectured on "intervention." Nor would we expect or accept the same outcome which this small band of gallant Cuban refugees must have known that they were chancing, determined as they were against heavy odds to pursue their courageous attempts to regain their Island's freedom. . . .

We will not accept Mr. [Fidel] Castro's attempts to blame this nation for the hatred with which his onetime supporters now regard his repression. But there are from this sobering episode useful lessons for us all to learn. Some may be still obscure, and await further information. Some are clear today.

Do Not Underestimate Communism

First, it is clear that the forces of communism are not to be underestimated, in Cuba or anywhere else in the world. The advantages of a police state—its use of mass terror and arrests to prevent the spread of free dissent—cannot be overlooked by those who expect the fall of every fanatic tyrant. If the self-discipline of the free cannot match the iron discipline of the mailed first—in economic, political, scientific and all the other kinds of struggles as well as the military—then the peril to freedom will continue to rise.

Cuba As the Seat of Global Communism

Secondly, it is clear that this Nation, in concert with all the free nations of this hemisphere, must take an ever closer and more realistic look at the menace of external Communist intervention and domination in Cuba. The American people are not complacent about Iron Curtain tanks and planes less than 90 miles from their shore. But a nation of Cuba's size is less a threat to our survival than it is a base for subverting the survival of other free nations throughout the hemisphere. It is not primarily our interest or our security

President Kennedy acknowledged the defeat at the Bay of Pigs but urged that the United States must continue to fight against communism.

but theirs which is now, today, in the greater peril. It is for their sake as well as our own that we must show our will.

The evidence is clear—and the hour is late. We and our Latin friends will have to face the fact that we cannot postpone any longer the real issue of survival of freedom in this hemisphere itself. On that issue, unlike perhaps some others, there can be no middle ground. Together we must build a hemisphere where freedom can flourish; and where any free nation under outside attack of any kind can be assured that all of our resources stand ready to respond to any request for assistance.

The Struggle to Defeat Communism Is Relentless

Third, and finally, it is clearer than ever that we face a relentless struggle in every corner of the globe that goes far beyond the clash of armies or even nuclear armaments. The armies are there, and in large number. The nuclear armaments are there. But they serve primarily as the shield behind which subversion, infiltration, and a host of other tactics steadily advance, picking off vulnerable areas one by one in situations which do not permit our own armed intervention.

> *The complacent, the self-indulgent, the soft societies are about to be swept away with the debris of history.*

Power is the hallmark of this offensive—power and discipline and deceit. The legitimate discontent of yearning people is exploited. The legitimate trappings of self-determination are employed. But once in power, all talk of discontent is repressed, all self-determination disappears, and the promise of a revolution of hope is betrayed, as in Cuba, into a reign of terror. . . .

We dare not fail to see the insidious nature of this new and deeper struggle. We dare not fail to grasp the new concepts, the new tools, the new sense of urgency we will need to combat it—whether in Cuba or South Viet-nam. And we dare not fail to realize that this struggle is taking place every day, without fanfare, in thousands of villages and markets—day and night—and in classrooms all over the globe.

The message of Cuba, of Laos, of the rising din of Communist voices in Asia and Latin America—these messages are all the same. The complacent, the self-indulgent, the soft societies are about to be swept away with the debris of history. Only the strong, only the industrious, only the determined, only the courageous, only the visionary who determine the real nature of our struggle can possibly survive.

Defending the World Against Communism Is Essential

No greater task faces this country or this administration. No other challenge is more deserving of our every effort and energy. Too long we have fixed our eyes on traditional military needs, on armies prepared to cross borders, on missiles poised for flight. Now it should be clear that this is no longer enough—that our security may be lost piece by piece, country by country, without the firing of a single missile or the crossing of a single border.

We intend to profit from this lesson. We intend to re-examine and reorient our forces of all kinds—our tactics and our institutions here in this community. We intend to intensify our efforts for a struggle in many ways more difficult than war, where disappointment will often accompany us.

For I am convinced that we in this country and in the free world possess the necessary resource, and the skill, and the added strength that comes from a belief in the freedom of man. And I am equally convinced that history will record the fact that this bitter struggle reached its climax in the late 1950's and the early 1960's. Let me then make clear as the President of the United States that I am determined upon our system's survival and success, regardless of the cost and regardless of the peril.

2

The United States Must Reexamine the Lessons of the Bay of Pigs

Stewart Alsop

Stewart Alsop, a well-known political writer and one-time contributing editor to the *Saturday Evening Post*, examines the failure at the Bay of Pigs in terms of the lessons that the U.S. government should have learned from the disaster. Published in June 1961, just two months after the invasion, his essay begins by questioning why the organizers of the invasion—capable and intelligent men—convinced themselves that Fidel Castro's regime could be easily toppled. The purpose of Alsop's essay is to explore this "mystery" and to explain what the U.S. government should learn from this failed strike. Alsop argues that there are four lessons to be learned. First, the men responsible for planning the Cuban invasion and other major operations should not be responsible for assessing the possible outcomes of such a major military action. Instead, people who are not involved with the operation should assess the probability of success and failure. Alsop reasons that, after all, these men are human beings who are invested in their projects and cannot rely on their own objectivity to properly evaluate their plans. Next, changing even one element of a major military plan requires that the whole plan be reevaluated. President John F. Kennedy's public announcements vowing that the United States would not involve its military in the Bay of Pigs invasion necessarily altered the original plans to commit U.S. air support and weapons. Unfortunately, the plan was not revised to take this new decision into account, and the result was disastrous. Lesson three, Alsop posits is that if a major military plan with so much at stake as the Bay of Pigs is to be undertaken, then the U.S. government must be willing to commit whatever resources it requires to see the action through to success, or else not undertake the operation at all. The fourth lesson, according to Alsop, is that the U.S. government should not try to carry out covert operations the way Communist governments do. Instead, the U.S. government must find its own way of attacking Communist oppression around the globe.

On the morning of April twentieth Fidel Castro's army was busy in the Bay of Pigs area, killing or capturing the pathetic remnants of the American-supported Cuban invasion force. That morning, when President [John F.] Kennedy rose to address a meeting of newspaper editors in Washington, he was in a grim, unsmiling mood.

"There are from this sobering episode useful lessons for us all to learn," he said. "Some may be still obscure and await further information. Some are clear today."

What lessons? And have we learned them?

Those questions need answering. For there was something downright mysterious about the whole Cuban disaster. The mystery is this. The President and his chief advisers are without exception intelligent men. Yet they mysteriously brought themselves to believe—almost unanimously, as we shall see—that a few hundred men could topple a well-entrenched Communist regime. And because they believed this, they permitted the prestige of the new Administration, and of the United States itself, to ride on the backs of those few hundred men. Surely this is mysterious.

The explanation of the mystery is a complex but fascinating story of human relationships, notably the relationship between the new President and the new men he brought into the Government, and the permanent professional military and civilian officials. It is not the purpose of this report to reconstruct the whole story of the Cuban disaster, although certain vital parts of the story which have not been told before will be told here. This report is, instead, an attempt to understand why certain astonishing errors in judgment were made, and why certain grievous faults in our Government's system of making decisions developed; and to suggest ways in which such faults might be corrected and such errors prevented from recurring in the future.

To this end, this reporter has talked at some length with most of the men in Washington who had a hand in the Cuban operation, and also with certain wise and thoughtful persons who were not involved. These talks suggest that there are four main "useful lessons" to be learned by hindsight from the Cuban disaster.

Lesson One: Objective Evaluators Are Crucial

The first is this: *The men responsible for mounting a major covert operation like the Cuban landings must not also be responsible for judging the operation's chances of success or failure.* Those chances must be assessed instead—and with a cold and fishy eye—by experts who are in no way involved in the operation, and who have their own independent sources of information.

To understand why this is so, it is first necessary to understand a simple fact. The men who run the special operations branch of the Central Intelligence Agency, which is the United States Government's "department of dirty tricks," are creatures of flesh and blood, even as you and I. Being human beings, they are capable of becoming emotionally involved in what they are doing, and this emotional involvement can in turn becloud their judgment.

The Cuban operation was, of course, a very big operation—by far the biggest of its kind the CIA had ever attempted. Thus many CIA men were involved.

There was something downright mysterious about the whole Cuban disaster.

But here it is necessary to mention only two names, which have already appeared in print, those of Allen Dulles, director of the CIA, and Richard M. Bissell, deputy for plans and operations. Dulles was in over-all charge of the Cuban operation, but Bissell ran it on a day-to-day basis.

Before going further, perhaps certain cards should be laid on the table. I have known and admired Allen Dulles for a good many years, and Richard Bissell is an old personal friend. So perhaps I am prejudiced. But I am certainly not alone in believing that both Dulles and Bissell are extraordinarily able, markedly intelligent and deeply dedicated to the national interest. How then did they—and all the other CIA men involved in the operation, many of them also able, intelligent and dedicated—go so wrong?

CIA Failure

For they did go wrong. There is no doubt on that score. It has been said that the CIA men stupidly thought that the Castro regime would simply disintegrate, like the walls of Jericho, with the first landing of anti-Castro troops. This is not true. But it is true that they firmly believed—and assured President Kennedy—that there would be sufficient uprisings and defections so that a beachhead could be held and expanded, and so that an anti-Castro government on Cuban soil could then be recognized and supported by the United States Government. Why were they so convinced that these things that did not happen, would happen?

The answer falls into three parts. First, there was a record of past success. It is unfashionable to say so, now that the CIA is the national whipping boy, but the CIA has had its share of successes. . . .

Such past successes gave the CIA men a dangerous confidence. So did their intelligence from Cuba. Almost without exception their operatives inside Cuba assured them that the hatred for Castro and his henchmen was so widespread that a majority of the Cuban people, given the means, would join an uprising against the bearded dictator.

Finally—and this was especially true of Bissell—the emotions of the CIA men who directed the Cuban operation became subtly and unconsciously engaged in the operation, and thus their judgment was clouded. It was quite natural that this should happen.

CIA Leaders Were Emotionally Involved

Almost a year before the landings, President [Dwight] Eisenhower had given the go-ahead signal for the training of a landing force of anti-Castro shock troops, from the men of military age among the more than 100,000 Cubans who had fled the Castro terror. Throughout that year the day-and-night preoccupation of Bissell and his subordinates had been the planning of the Cuban landings. Inevitably, being human, they had become infected with something of the fervor, the courage and the false optimism of the Cuban refugees, who were willing to bet their lives . . . on the proposition that the hated Castro could be brought down: Is it any wonder that the CIA men became, instead of coolly skeptical judges of the chances of success of the operation, its passionate partisans?

That, in any case, is that they did become. "Allen and Dick didn't just brief us on the Cuban operation," says one of President Kennedy's White House advisers. "They sold us on it." It is always difficult to distinguish between fact and self-exoneration when an official is employing twenty-twenty hindsight. But in this case there is no doubt that the CIA men responsible for mounting the Cuban operation did become its eloquent advocates.

Moreover, although the machinery for examining the operation with that much-needed coldly critical eye did exist within the CIA itself, in the board of "national estimates," the machinery was never used. Official knowledge of the operation was limited to its sponsors, on a "need-to-know" basis. The net effect was that the operational CIA men sat in judgment of their own much-loved offspring.

There is no doubt that the CIA men responsible for . . . the Cuban operation did become its eloquent advocates.

By the same token, the military men who were responsible for the detailed planning of the landing also sat in judgment on their own handiwork. The CIA employs many military men, and others were assigned by the Pentagon to help plan the Cuban invasion. The plans they evolved were reviewed in detail by the Joint Staff, top planning board under the august Joint Chiefs of Staff, and then by two of the chiefs, Gen. Lyman Lemnitzer, Chairman of the Joint Chiefs, and Adm. Arleigh Burke, Chief of Naval Operations.

Lemnitzer and Burke strongly endorsed the plans, in writing, to the President, on two conditions—that the CIA's political estimate was correct, and that the anti-Castro forces would control the air over the battlefield. As in the case of the CIA, the enthusiasm of the military for their own plans was at least understandable. A military man, asked to devise a plan to achieve a given objective, naturally becomes a partisan of the plan he has evolved. The military have in any case a natural proclivity for action as against inaction—excessive caution ill becomes a soldier.

Kennedy Was Misled

But again, among the military there were none to assay the operation's chances of success with that much-needed cold and fishy eye. On the contrary, President Kennedy was assured by the Joint Chiefs as well as by the CIA that the Cuban adventure had a better chance of success than the successful anti-Communist operation in Guatemala.

"It never did smell right to the President," one of his aides says.

Now consider President Kennedy's position, when, after his election, he found on his desk the Top Secret plan for a Cuban landing operation evolved under the Administration of his predecessor. Here is a new President, more experienced in the matter of winning primaries than judging the likelihood of success of a covert operation. He finds that all the professionals in this secret business, *without a single exception*, favor an operation which, if it succeeds, will greatly alter the situation in the Western Hemisphere in favor of the United States. He finds that nearly 3000 Cubans have been trained by the U.S. Government, with at least an implicit assurance that they will be helped by that Government to liberate their homeland from a Communist tyrant. The President is told, moreover, that time is running out. Soviet jet fighters are arriving in crates in Cuba. Czech-trained Cuban pilots are due there soon, and the Guatemalan Government had given notice that the Cuban training camps in Guatemala must soon be evacuated. Suppose the President cancels the operation. Won't the Cubans—and a lot of other people, including Republicans—say then that the new President chickened out, that he lost the last chance to knock off Castro? And what is more, Kennedy must have asked himself, *Might they not be right?*

On one point all witnesses agree. From the start Kennedy's interest was to kill the operation. "It never did smell right to the President," one of his aides says. After the disaster Kennedy took full responsibility for what had happened. Under our system that is precisely where the final responsibility belongs. But with all the old pros favoring the operation, it is not hard to understand why Kennedy did not follow his own instincts and cancel the operation.

Kennedy Relied on His Own Men

What he did instead was to turn from the old pros—the CIA professionals and the military—to the new boys, the men he himself had brought into the Government. He turned especially to Dean Rusk, his Secretary of State, and to his able special assistant, McGeorge Bundy. These men should have supplied that much-needed cold and fishy eye. They did not and again for a humanly understandable reason.

Both Rusk and Bundy—especially the former—had the same instinctive doubts about the operation that Kennedy had. As in Kennedy's case, the notion that a thousand or so refugees could bring down Castro didn't smell right, and the risks appeared to them to be very great. And yet, again like Kennedy himself, they were impressed by the solid phalanx of professionals who all but promised success. Who were they to say that the experienced and respected Dulles or the four-starred Lemnitzer were talking through their hats?

Other Kennedy appointees who were consulted, like South American expert Adolf Berle, had the same instinctive hesitations and the same instinctive disinclination to take on the old pros of the CIA and the Pentagon. Under Secretary of State Chester Bowles wrote a memorandum to his chief, Dean Rusk, expressing reservations, but the memorandum was strictly "in channels," and it is doubtful if the President ever saw it. The President did see a memorandum written for him by his controversial assistant, Prof. Arthur Schlesinger, flatly opposing the scheme.

A man watches his tongue and his step when he is speaking in the presence of the President.

Schlesinger, who had had experience as a desk officer in the wartime Office of Strategic Services, had learned to be skeptical of intelligence estimates based on the hopes of refugees. He also feared the global political consequences of a failure in Cuba, or even a partial success. But Schlesinger is far down the pecking order and, although he did express his doubts in his memorandum to the President, he was chary of opposing the scheme in meetings. "Arthur was right, all right." says one participant, "but he was mighty quiet about it."

This quietness, this reluctance to speak out in meetings,

was another intangible factor which led Kennedy in the end to give the operation a half-hearted green light. When Kennedy had been a senator and a candidate, he and his small band of political aides used to sit around in shirt sleeves, feet up, plotting, planning and arguing interminably with one another far into the night. "They reminded me of Robin Hood and his merry men," one Kennedy intimate has said. In those days Robin Hood Kennedy was always certain to hear the pros and cons of any course of action argued loudly and at length.

Kennedy tried to introduce the same note of argumentative informality into the White House. But now he was no longer Robin Hood, and his advisers were no longer his merry men, old friends who knew one another like a band of brothers. He was President of the United States, encased in that "divinity that doth hedge a king," and many of his advisers had until recently been strangers to him and to each other. A man watches his tongue and his step when he is speaking in the presence of the President. In that presence a prudent man does not lightly oppose other men, who represent immensely powerful interests, for opposition is often interpreted as hostility. And especially in an Administration billed as "young, dynamic and vigorous," an ambitious official does not like to be placed in the position of favoring inaction over action.

The Need for Suspicion

For all these reasons the operators were allowed to sit in judgment on their own operation, and the operation was never really subjected to the attentions of that necessary cold and fishy eye. . . .

But suppose there were a small, competent staff of people who really knew where the more important bodies were buried. . . . Suppose it was the function of these people to act as prodders, skeptics and naysayers, to ask the embarrassing questions about any proposed course of action—or, what can be just as important, any inaction. In that case there might be a better chance that the President would really see the whole picture before he made up his mind, and thus a better chance to avoid such avoidable disasters as that in Cuba.

What actually happened, when the President weighed the views of the new boss against those of the old pros, was that a peculiar, progressive watering-down process occurred. In the end, as a result of this process, the Cuban plan that was put into operation was different in essential ways from the plan Kennedy had inherited from Eisenhower.

That plan, like the final Kennedy plan, was based on the assumption that there would be widespread anti-Castro uprisings and defections. It was hoped that these would make any overt American military intervention unnecessary. But the Eisenhower plan also envisaged American intervention on a "contingency basis." American aircraft would intervene, either openly or in unmarked planes, if necessary to maintain control over the beachhead and prevent destruction of the anti-Castro forces.

But, [Kennedy] ruled, under no circumstances whatever would American forces become involved.

From the very first this was the aspect of the Cuban plan which Kennedy and most of his new boys disliked most heartily. By early March, on Kennedy's insistence, an alternative plan had been devised. This plan called for air strikes against Castro's air force. The air strikes were to be billed for world consumption as the work of defectors from the Castro air force, but were actually to be mounted from Guatemalan bases and piloted by Cuban refugee pilots. These air strikes were to knock out the Castro air force, pathetically small by Pentagon standards, and thus obviate any need for American intervention. The new plan had been vetted and approved by the Pentagon and the CIA. But the final decisions were taken at two crucial meetings, on April fourth and April fifth. . . .

At [the second] meeting Kennedy made his final decision to go ahead with the operation. But, he ruled, under no circumstances whatever would American forces become involved. Moreover, the Cuban leaders must be categorically warned in advance of this decision. . . . The Cuban Leaders . . . unanimously opted to go ahead with the plan regardless. And thus the disaster drew closer.

Clearly the President's ruling against American armed intervention under any circumstances—short of a Castro attack on the Guantanamo base—constituted a basic change in the whole nature of the operation. To an extent, the change was recognized, and taken into account. . . .

In fact, although changes were made in the plan in the light of the President's decision, no one really asked the key question: "If the United States is not willing to ensure success, should a comparative handful of Cuban refugees be permitted nevertheless to risk American prestige on a venture which clearly might fail?"

Lesson Two: The Cuban Plan Needed to Be Reevaluated

One reason there was no really searching re-examination of the plan was the fact that no one wanted to be in the position of saying: "If the President refuses to take any risk of committing American forces, then the whole operation ought to be called off." This is not the sort of thing an ambitious public official likes to say. Another reason is that there is a kind of built-in glacial inertia in any really major Government operation, which makes it terribly difficult to reverse the gears and call the operation off. In any case, the second lesson of the Cuban tragedy is surely clear: *If a vital chance is made in the plan for a major operation like the Cuban adventure, then the whole plan must be re-examined* de novo, *from start to finish, and again with that cold and fishy eye.*

When President Kennedy gave the green light to the operation with the proviso that American forces could never be used, he was indulging in the agreeable but dangerous pastime of trying to eat his cake and have it too. Two decisions made just as the operation was being mounted derived from the same tendency.

Encouraging an Anti-Castro Uprising

First, a few days before the invasion took place the President said flatly at a press conference what he had already decided privately—that the United States would under no circumstances intervene with force in Cuba. The decision to make this public announcement, which neatly tied the President's own hands in advance, derived from a desire to "preserve the American image." But the whole object of the Cuban exercise was to spark a general anti-Castro uprising.

There were many reasons why there were never even the beginnings of such an uprising, including poor liaison with the anti-Castro underground and the unexpected efficiency of Castro's Communist-trained secret police. But one reason, surely, was the President's public promise that under no circumstances would the United States lift a finger to help the anti-Castro forces. Put yourself in the position of an anti-Castro Cuban. If you were assured in advance that the United States intended to take no chances to ensure Castro's downfall, you would be strongly disinclined to take any chances either.

The Failure to Destroy Castro's Air Force

Another have-your-cake-and-eat-it-too decision was taken just on the eve of the landings. As we have seen, an essential part of the Kennedy plan was the knocking out of Castro's tiny air force by the sixteen Guatemala-based B-26 bombers supplied to the rebels by the CIA. The first air strike occurred on April fifteenth, two days before the landings. According to plan, it was billed as a spontaneous act by pilots defecting from Castro's air force. . . .

As the invaders were soon tragically to learn, three armed T-33 jet trainer . . . had survived. The comparatively lumbering B-26s of the invading forces were sitting ducks for the jets. The invaders' ammunition ship, the *Rio Escondido*, was sunk, and the invaders soon lost what all the planners had recognized as essential—control of the air over the battlefield. When that was lost, all was lost.

Lesson Three: Support Is Essential

This surely suggests the third lesson of the Cuban disaster: *We must recognize that this kind of major operation, with great prizes at stake, cannot be done on the cheap. If the price of failure is too high—as it was in Cuba—we must have the will and the means to prevent failure. Otherwise, the operation should not be undertaken at all.*

No doubt the chances are high that the eventual outcome would have been the same if the President had not announced his decision to bar all American intervention, and then canceled the second strike against the Castro air force. But the lesson remains clear. You cannot mount a covert operation designed to destroy a foreign regime you dislike and at the same time maintain that air of virginal innocence which American officials, especially our spokesman at the UN, so love to wear. . . .

By the evening of April eighteenth it was clear that the invasion would be crushed, short of American intervention to regain control of the air over the beachhead. The President, summoned from a white-tie party, stayed up until the small hours of the morning of April nineteenth arguing the pros and cons of intervention. . . . Still undecided, he called a meeting of all his key advisers for the next day.

Kennedy's First Great Failure

The meeting must have been an agonizing one, for almost all those present had a measure of personal responsibility for the bloody tragedy then being acted out in the Bay of Pigs. In the end, partly because he had already tied his own hands and partly because it was by then too late, the President decided to do nothing.

That decision marked the first great Kennedy failure. Bobby Kennedy, who hates failure more even than most Kennedys, was present. He remarked as the sad meeting ended, that what worried him most was that now nobody in the Government would be willing to stick his neck out, to take a chance, to plan bold and aggressive action against the Communists.

Surely the President's brother was essentially right. If the Communists are permitted indefinitely to retain their present monopoly of the techniques of the oblique thrust, the invasion by proxy, they will win in the end all over the world, as they are winning now in Southeast Asia. Moreover, the hatred of Communist oppression within the Communist states—Cuba included—is surely the West's essential asset in the long struggle in which we are now engaged. Ways must be found to exploit that asset.

In Cuba we tried to use Communist ways, not American ways, to exploit the asset. . . . Our kind of society, with a free people and a free press, simply does not permit the iron discipline and total secrecy required for a Communist-type exercise in subversion. But does this mean that our hands are forever tied? . . .

Lesson Four: The United States Must Do Battle in Its Own Way

The fourth lesson of Cuba seems to be something like this:

We cannot permit the Communist bloc to enjoy a monopoly of the techniques of the oblique thrust. But we must find our own ways, deriving from our own past and our own kind of society, for carrying the battle to the Communists.

3

The Bay of Pigs Decisions Had Long- Term Effects on U.S. Foreign Policy

Walter LaFeber

In the following essay Walter LaFeber, a noted historian and professor of history at Cornell University, argues that the U.S. government did not understand how best to deal with Cuban leader Fidel Castro in the early 1960s. LaFeber begins by discussing the U.S. involvement in Cuba before Castro took power. From 1898 through the end of dictator Fulgencio Batista's reign on New Year's Day in 1959, the United States had control of Cuba. When Castro came to power, he sought to return the control of Cuba to the Cuban government. Under the direction of President Dwight Eisenhower, the U.S. government imposed tough economic restrictions on Cuba, attempting to force Castro to stop trying to free Cuba from what he considered U.S. imperialism. When President John F. Kennedy took office in 1961, he inherited the Cuba problem. Firmly believing that anti-Castro Cubans would take up arms and fight once the antirevolutionaries landed on the beaches, Kennedy sent in troops of U.S.-trained Cuban refugees. According to LaFeber, Kennedy's hatred of Castro and his fear of being seen as less of an anti-Communist than Eisenhower, his former presidential opponent, led to this poorly devised plan that was destined to fail. In contrast with other historians, who believe the failure of the Bay of Pigs was caused by the poor strategy of the CIA and military experts, LaFeber blames the U.S. government's misunderstanding of the causes of revolu-

Walter LaFeber, "The Unlearned Lessons: Lest We Forget the Bay of Pigs," *The Nation*, vol. 242, April 19, 1986, p. 537. Copyright © 1986 by The Nation magazine/The Nation Company, Inc. Reproduced by permission.

tion. He argues that instead of dealing with the causes of the Cuban revolution—both political and economical—Kennedy was more interested in dealing with the effects, namely the spread of communism and the loss of U.S. control of Cuba. This distorted emphasis on the effects of the Communist revolution led not only to the embarrassing defeat at the Bay of Pigs but also continued to affect the ways in which the United States conducted foreign policy in subsequent decades.

P resident Kennedy's attempt to destroy Fidel Castro's regime at the Bay of Pigs has rightly been called the perfect failure. But the debacle of April 17, 1961, went far beyond Cuba. It helped lure the United States down a violent dead-end street in pursuit of revolutionaries throughout Latin America. It resulted in the first Soviet presence in the hemisphere. It rapidly accelerated Washington's disastrous policies in Vietnam. It caused nations throughout the world to question U.S. judgment and dependability. Twenty-five years later Washington officials still do not understand the reasons for this failure and seem bent on repeating it.

> *When in early 1960 the United States tried to strangle Castro with tough economic sanctions, he turned to the Soviet bloc for help.*

Certainly no place appeared more vulnerable to U.S. power than Cuba. The United States had controlled the island since 1898. Its ambassador was Cuba's second-most-powerful official, after the president, and at times the most powerful. Fidel Castro changed all that with his victory over dictator Fulgencio Batista on New Year's Day, 1959. During the rest of that year, his determination to transform Cuba led to radical land reforms and other economic changes that brought him closer to the Cuban Communist Party—which, as late as 1958, had refused to work with him—and put him on a collision course with the Eisenhower Administration. . . .

Guatemala and Nicaragua Offer Aid

When in early 1960 the United States tried to strangle Castro with tough economic sanctions, he turned to the Soviet bloc for help. Eisenhower tightened the choke hold and, in March of that year, secretly ordered the Central Intelligence Agency to plan an invasion of Cuba. U.S. appeals for help in isolating Cuba drew little response from Latin American countries, who feared the Cubans less than Washington's century-old policy of intervention in their affairs. But two dependable friends did volunteer: Guatemalan dictator Gen. Miguel Ydigoras, one in a succession of military leaders who ruled that country after the C.I.A. overthrew the elected reformist government in 1954, and Anastasio Somoza in Nicaragua. Those two men provided training bases in their countries for the Cuban exiles involved in the Bay of Pigs operation. This collaboration is indelibly etched in Central American and Cuban memories.

Kennedy Takes Control

Campaigning for the presidency in 1960, Kennedy blamed Eisenhower for losing Cuba to the Communists. The accusation trapped the new President. He discovered that the former general, an old hand at plotting covert counterrevolutions, had invasion plans well under way. Kennedy's State Department, however, warned that such an incursion would set back U.S. relations with Latin America and, moreover, probably fail. It quickly became obvious that the C.I.A.'s plans were lacking in intelligence, in both senses of the word. The agency and the Administration said openly that Cuban exiles were going to restore freedom to their homeland, but clearly the C.I.A. was recruiting, training and controlling them. Mutual trust was conspicuously absent. . . . Propaganda about the exiles made U.S. officials believe that the invasion, carried out by an independently formed anti-Castro force, would cost this country almost nothing. The ultimate responsibility lay with the C.I.A. and Kennedy. Both desperately tried to ignore the operation's central problem—North Americans telling the Cubans how to run their country—by assuming that once the exile force landed, the Cuban people would spontaneously assist in overthrowing Castro.

Harboring serious reservations about the operation, Kennedy decided to cut direct U.S. military support to an absolute minimum. Nevertheless, he despised Castro and saw himself going head-to-head with [Soviet premier] Nikita Khrushchev over which superpower would control the Third World. He was also passionately committed to a romantic view of counterrevolutionary operations and feared being labeled as less of an anti-Communist than Eisenhower, whose policies he had blasted only months earlier. So the attack went ahead on the night of April 17.

Kennedy Accepts
Responsibility for the Failure

It was doomed from the start. In the first place, the C.I.A. mistook the coral reefs in the Bay of Pigs for seaweed. The exile crafts ran aground and were easy targets for Castro's small but effective air force. When U.S. naval officers on an aircraft carrier just offshore urgently requested permission to launch their planes to support the exiles, the White House rejected the request. Robert Kennedy recalled: "We kept asking when the uprisings were going to take place. Dick Bissell [the C.I.A. official in charge of the operation] said it was going to take place during the night. Of course no uprising did take place." Castro killed or captured nearly all the invaders. At a televised press conference Kennedy took full responsibility for the disaster.

It was doomed from the start.

Kennedyites have since gone to great lengths to blame the fiasco on the C.I.A. But deeper causes than agency bungling were involved. In the aftermath, U.S. officials tried to fool the public into believing that the exile force was acting on its own and that it was so strongly identified with the cause of freedom that the Cuban people would rally to its banner. Those officials were, and remain, vastly ignorant of both the damage North American control has inflicted on Caribbean and Central American societies and the promise of escape from that past that revolutionaries like Castro seemed to offer.

Moreover, the exiles could never have conquered Castro's army without massive U.S. involvement. That realization led Senator J. William Fulbright, in a last-ditch attempt to stop the invasion, to pose the classic question: What if we win? "Winning" would have meant a U.S. occupation of Cuba and, no doubt, a bloody guerilla war. U.S. troops in Cuba would have been as unpopular as the Russians are in Afghanistan. In addition, most Americans took seriously the U.S. commitment to the Organization of American States Charter of 1948 not to use force to overthrow Latin American governments. As it was, the invasion violated that pledge. The respect for the rule of law that supposedly distinguishes U.S. foreign policy from that of the Soviet Union was cast aside.

Vietnam and the Bay of Pigs

Kennedy's successors have continued to regard the Bay of Pigs tragedy as a failure by the "experts" to run a military operation properly, instead of what it was: a failure to understand the political and economic causes of revolution. By relying on the C.I.A. and the exiles, U.S. officials unwittingly tried to revive the imperialist past. Over the next several years Kennedy's Administration authorized sabotage, dirty tricks and even assassination attempts to eliminate Castro. Those attacks only made the Cuban leader more popular at home and drove him closer to the Russians. Finally, in the aftermath of the debacle, Kennedy resolved to redeem himself by sending more troops to Vietnam. The significant escalation of involvement in Southeast Asia by the end of 1961 was a direct result of Kennedy's misreading of the lessons to be drawn from the Cuban revolution. With the Bay of Pigs invasion Kennedy dealt militarily with the effects, not the causes, of revolution.

Important Figures in the Bay of Pigs

Fulgencio Batista, semi-constitutional ruler (1940–1944) and dictator of Cuba from 1952 until Fidel Castro overthrew his office on New Year's Eve 1959. He fled to the Dominican Republic and then to Spain, where he lived in exile until his death in 1973.

Richard M. Bissell Jr., deputy director for plans, CIA, from 1959 until he was fired by President John F. Kennedy in February 1962.

Chester Bowles, under secretary of state, 1961 through 1963.

McGeorge Bundy, special assistant to the president for national security, 1961 through 1966.

Arleigh A. Burke, chief of Naval Operations, 1955 through 1961. He is known for holding this position for more consecutive terms than any other incumbent.

C.P. Cabell, deputy director, CIA, until he was fired by President John F. Kennedy in 1962.

Fidel Castro, premier (since 1959) and president of the Cuban Republic (since 1976). In the early 1950s he practiced law in Havana, Cuba, and attempted to run for Parliament. In 1956, along with Cuban exiles known as the Twenty-sixth of July Revolutionary Movement, Castro attempted to overthrow Fulgencio Batista's government and lost. The surviving members returned on New Year's Eve 1959 and were successful.

Allen Dulles, director, CIA, 1953 through 1961.

Alfredo Duran, early member of Brigade 2506. After the invasion failed, he spent thirty days in a Cuban swamp and was eventually captured by Castro's troops.

Dwight D. Eisenhower, U.S. president from 1953 through 1961. The Bay of Pigs plans were developed during his presidency.

Jacob D. Esterline, CIA chief of branch 4, a Guatemalan station, 1954 through 1957.

Miguel Ydigoras Fuentes, president of Guatemala from 1958 until he was overthrown in 1963. He granted permission to the CIA to train its anti-Castro militia in preparation for the Bay of Pigs invasion in his country.

Ernesto "Che" Guevara, revolutionary leader and Castro's close companion. He was shot and killed in Bolivia in 1967 while trying to help the Bolivian people overthrow their government.

Jack Hawkins, chief of Paramilitary Operations, Branch 4, Western Hemisphere Division, Directorate of Plans, CIA.

Lyndon B. Johnson, vice president of the United States under President Kennedy. He became president in 1963, following Kennedy's death.

John F. Kennedy, U.S. president from January 1961 until November 1963.

Robert F. Kennedy, U.S. attorney general (1961–1963) and brother of John F. Kennedy. He was assassinated in 1968 during his run for presidency.

Nikita S. Khrushchev, chairman of the Council of Ministers of the USSR from 1958 until his ouster in 1964.

Lyman Kirkpatrick, inspector general, CIA, until 1965. All but one copy of his scathing report of the failure at the Bay of Pigs was destroyed and remained classified until 1998.

Lyman L. Lemnitzer, chairman of the Joint Chiefs of Staff, 1960 through 1962.

Richard M. Nixon, presidential candidate in 1960, vice president of the United States under President Dwight D. Eisenhower, 1953 through 1961. He became president in 1968 and won a second term in 1972, only to serve two years before resigning.

Erneido Oliva, deputy commander, Brigade 2506.

Rene Vallejo Ortiz, personal aide to Castro.

José "Pepe" Peréz San Ramón, commander, Brigade 2506.

Dean Rusk, U.S. secretary of state, 1952 through 1961.

Carlos Rodriguez Santana, Brigade 2506 was named after his military number. He was the first casualty of the exile force when he was killed during a training accident in Guatemala.

Arthur M. Schlesinger Jr., special assistant to President John F. Kennedy.

Adlai E. Stevenson, U.S. permanent representative at the United Nations, 1961 through 1965.

Walter C. Sweeney, commander in chief, Tactical Air Command.

For Further Research

Books

Richard M. Bissell Jr., *Reflections of a Cold Warrior: From Yalta to the Bay of Pigs*. New Haven, CT: Yale University Press, 1996.

James G. Blight and Peter Kornbluh, eds., *Politics of Illusion: The Bay of Pigs Invasion Reexamined*. Boulder, CO: Lynne Rienner, 1998.

Trumbull Higgins, *The Perfect Failure: Kennedy, Eisenhower, and the C.I.A. at the Bay of Pigs*. New York: Norton, 1987.

Haynes Johnson et al., *The Bay of Pigs: The Leaders' Story of Brigade 2506*. New York: Norton, 1964.

Grayston L. Lynch, *Decision for Disaster: Betrayal at the Bay of Pigs*. Washington, DC: Brassey's, 1998.

Operation Zapata: The "Ultrasensitive" Report and Testimony of the Board of Inquiry on the Bay of Pigs. Frederick, MD: Aletheia Books and University Publications of America, 1981.

Albert C. Persons, *Bay of Pigs*. Birmingham, AL: Kingston, 1968.

Juan Carlos Rodriguez, *The Bay of Pigs and the CIA*. Trans. Mary Todd Melbourne. New York: Ocean, 1999.

Warren Trest and Don Dodd, *Wings of Denial: The Alabama Air National Guard's Covert Role at the Bay of Pigs*. Montgomery, AL: New South Books, 2001.

Mark J. White, ed., *The Kennedys and Cuba: The Declassified Documentary History*. Chicago: Ivan R. Dee, 1999.

Peter Wyden, *Bay of Pigs: The Untold Story*. New York: Simon and Schuster, 1979.

Periodicals

Jeffrey D. Bass, "Beyond the Bay of Pigs: The Cuban Volunteer Program and the Reorientation of Anti-Castroism," *Historian*, Winter 2000.

Don Bohning, "Bay of Pigs Veteran Says Only Military Can Rid Island of Castro," Knight Ridder/Tribune News Service, April 14, 2000.

Max Castro, "Have We Learned Anything?" *Miami Herald*, January 18, 2001.

Piero Gleijeses, "Ships in the Night: The CIA, the White House, and the Bay of Pigs," *Journal of Latin American Studies*, February 1995.

Daniel Schorr, "In Havana, Old Foes Come Together for a Bay of Pigs Reunion," *Christian Science Monitor*, March 30, 2001.

Internet Sources

Cubasocialista, "Playa Giron," 2002. www.cubasocialista. com/Bay0.html.

J.A. Sierra, "Invasion at Bay of Pigs," April 2003. www. historyofcuba.com/history/baypigs/pigs.htm.

Michael Warner, "Lessons Unlearned: The CIA's Internal Probe of the Bay of Pigs Affair," Winter 1998–1999. www.cia.gov/csi/studies/winter98-99/art08.html.

Websites

The Bay of Pigs Invasion, www.rose-hulman.edu/~delacova/baypigs.htm.

The Bay of Pigs Invasion: Brigade 2506, www.brigade2506. com.

Playagirón.org, http://playagiron.org/pg.

Videos

The Bay of Pigs. Written, directed, and produced by David Davis. Alexandria, VA: PBS Video, 1997.

Conflict in Cuba: Bay of Pigs and Cuban Missile Crisis. Produced by CBS News Productions, in association with the History Channel. New York: History Channel Video and A&E Home Video, 1998.

Dateline—1961, Cuba. Northbrook, IL: MTI Film & Video, 1989.

From the Bay of Pigs to the Brink. Princeton, NJ: Films for the Humanities & Sciences, 1991.

Index